Happy christmas D☺addy

with LOaDS !!! of

Love

charlie xxxxxx xx xx xxxxxx xx x xx xxxxxxxxx

♡ ♡ ♡ ♡ ♡

2009

THE OAKS

OF CHEVITHORNE BARTON

THE OAKS
OF CHEVITHORNE BARTON

Michael Heathcoat Amory

Adelphi Publishers

The Oaks of Chevithorne Barton

Published by
Adelphi Publishers
10 Northburgh St
London EC1V 0AT

Text © 2009 Michael Heathcoat Amory
Photographs © 2009 James MacEwen

ISBN 978-0-9562387-0-2

Designed by Anikst Design, London
Printed and bound in Germany

All rights reserved. No part of this publication
may be reproduced, stored in a retrieval
system or transmitted, in any form or by any
means, electronic, mechanical, photocopying,
recording or otherwise, without the prior
written permission of the copyright owners.

frontispiece: autumn growth on

Q. obtusata x *Q. rugosa*

Contents

Every so often something wonderful happens. So it was, when I received a letter from Michael Heathcoat Amory, asking if I would contribute a foreword to the book he was preparing about his oak collection.

The existence of such a book was not a surprise for I have shared the excitement of Michael's remarkable passion for this most fascinating genus of trees and shrubs since its inception a quarter of a century ago. Indeed for much of the journey, we have marched step by step, as year by year, we added yet more names to our respective catalogues. Slowly but surely Michael's collection drew ahead as his specialisation and energy drove him to explore every nook and cranny for acorn, cutting or growing plant. It was a joy to visit and to salute his professionalism. As he freely admits, it was not always so, as overcrowded plantings, mislabelling and youthful exuberance delivered the inevitable lessons.

But if the invitation brought a personal thrill at an association with so prestigious a project, the proofs of the book were impressive. This is a template for the perfect reference book. Page after page of clear informative photographs with concise descriptions, checked by some of the leading authorities and collectors of our time.

Michael's name will live over the centuries for the legacy he will leave at Chevithorne Barton. It is, without question, one of the great horticultural achievements of our time. This book records the first quarter century. Two hundred years or more of English arboricultural history is now taking root in this renowned Devon garden.

The Rt Hon the Lord Heseltine CH
March 2009

Quercus monimotricha,
watercolour by Christine Battle

For Arabella

I have been collecting oaks in my spare time for twenty-five years. This book describes both how the collection at Chevithorne Barton was created and its current range. Of the 382 different sorts of named oak now in the collection, 190 of the more notable are here described, most of which are illustrated. It will be obvious that I have had a massive amount of help, which was given freely by so many people. They are acknowledged in the book but if I have missed any out, I can only apologise.

This book could not have been produced without very considerable help from Elizabeth Watts. I am most grateful to Allen Coombes, current President of the International Oak Society, who wrote the technical descriptions and much more, and to James MacEwen who took almost all the photographs and helped to drive the book along. I am indebted to Professor Richard Jensen for his most valuable and learned contribution to the text and to Piers Trehane, the Registrar for oak names for the International Oak Society, who has so ably edited the final text of this book. However the responsibility for its contents remains mine.

When I started to collect, I did so because oaks had such variety, and encompass so many outstanding species, and also because oaks through the ages have been of vital importance to man in so many different ways. I thought then it would be an interesting, if challenging, genus to collect and a quarter of a century later I have not changed my mind.

Michael Heathcoat Amory
Chevithorne Barton
February 2009

Chevithorne Barton is a late Elizabethan manor-house deep in the Devonshire countryside. It is on a south facing hillside surrounded by gardens, orchards, woods and fields. It has fairly high rainfall and good soil and several streams and leats which are useful in dry weather. Its name derives from 'Ciffa's Thorntree', and is mentioned in the *Domesday Book*. The core of the current house was built for the Francis family in 1610, although several parts have been destroyed and rebuilt since then. It was bought by Sir John Heathcoat Amory in 1905, and he handed it to his youngest son, Ludovic, my grandfather, when he married in 1911. His wife was Mary 'May' Stuart Bannatyne, whose family owned a successful milling business in Limerick, but whose father lived at Haldon Hall near Exeter.

The garden was an important part of their plans for the house from the moment they bought it. Letters that Ludy, as he was known, wrote to my grandmother from the front line during the First World War contain constant references to the garden and their ideas for it. In October 1917, he wrote: 'I wish I'd seen our Michaelmas daisies at their best. I always love them with the little Jap anemones.' But he was killed in August 1918, and all of my grandmother's three sons – including my father, Gerald – met the same fate during the Second World War. My grandmother was therefore alone at Chevithorne Barton for large periods of her life. Partly because of her rather tragic history, she threw herself into gardening and developed a notable plantswoman's garden with the emphasis on rock gardens, herbaceous borders and plants that grow well in woods. She planted some fine trees and shrubs, notably a large tulip tree and a *Magnolia ×veitchii* which can be seen flowering from 3 miles away in the spring. Her generation of gardeners included Margery Fish and Lanning Roper, who reputedly got some of his early inspiration from her garden.

In 1960 Lanning Roper wrote an article in *Country Life* about the gardens at Chevithorne Barton, which he said 'embody all the elements with which my ideal garden is endowed.' He went on to praise 'an abundance of flowers which grow with an exuberance and luxuriance which gladden the heart of every gardener... the highly successful integration of the garden not only with the house and farm buildings, around which the gardens are laid out, but with the lovely Devon landscape...[and] lastly the ample water.' He noted the 'lily pond embraced by two curving flights of flower carpeted steps, a gently flowing stream with reflections of purple nuts, golden laburnums and the apple blossoms of the orchard through which it flows.'

Above all, he loved the 'controlled abandon that makes this garden romantic, informal, completely satisfying and above all else unique.' Roper then went on to give a full – and fulsome – description of the

garden, which it seems worth quoting at some length because it explains the garden that I inherited when I moved to the house in 1967, and describes a basic structure which I have kept and which has stood the test of time. To the east of the house, Roper described: 'a series of terraces. The stone work of the steps, paths, walls and garden house on the top terrace are so overgrown with erigerons, campanulas, thymes, and endless other rock plants that all rigidity has been lost and there is a mellow softness, not only of the structural lines but of the stone itself, with its coating of moss and lichens.'

The terraces had been built by hand in the 1930s, closely supervised by my grandmother. A photograph from the time shows the work in progress, as she created a complex terraced garden from a grassy slope. Continuing down the hill, Roper described how 'an iron gate reveals a charming vista of shrubbery and orchard on the slopes beyond. A path leads down the slope, first through masses of peonies, heathers, hydrangeas, azaleas and berberis growing in the shade of laburnums, lilacs, amelanchiers and apple trees, in pleasant contrast to the intensively gardened area of the terraces.'

Further down the hill, Roper reached 'an enchanted woodland garden', 'not large in extent but owing to the simple plan of the winding paths and open vistas it seems far larger than it is. There is a delightful mixture of larch, pines and silver birch.' Next to the wood was the kitchen garden, of which the centrepiece was 'wide central herbaceous borders flanking a well kept grass panel path, which terminates in a handsome Italian well head, flanked by slender poplars, planted against a tapestry of mixed beach hedge.'

In the 1970s I took out the herbaceous borders but my wife, Arabella, and I have since reinstated them with 'espaliered fruit trees' and relocated the 'neat blocks of vegetables and soft fruit' to another location, to the west of the house. Roper clearly loved the garden, with its 'wealth of flowers and rich scents... roses, honeysuckle, cherry pie and mignonette... great drifts of anemones... huge white chalices of magnolias and the green architectural splendour of a large well placed yucca.'

This was the garden that, as May's only grandson, I inherited at the age of 25 in 1966. To begin with, I rather resented the legacy and, in particular, the cost of the two or three gardeners whom she employed. As time went on, however, I got more and more enthusiastic but in the garden the emphasis switched to trees and shrubs: we planted magnolias (including yellow ones and michelias), rhododendrons, hamamelis, eucryphias and many others.

The start of the collection

The first named oaks were planted nearly ten years later in the garden which then amounted to about five hectares (12.3 acres). It was not long before it became obvious that the garden was not big enough so the planting area was extended to orchards, small woods and fields adjacent to the garden, which had the effect of virtually encircling the house. From the beginning, some trees were planted deliberately in exposed positions but in full sunlight, while others were planted in sheltered conditions, very often with restricted sunlight. Some are planted in damp or well watered positions, some on dry banks. There has been no real pattern as to which has worked best, but some of the best specimens of delicate Mexican oaks have grown in the old Rifle Range, in full sunlight but exposed to wind, especially from the south east, yet also benefiting from a leat which runs along the whole length of the Rifle Range and which leaks just enough to provide a natural irrigation system in dry summers.

To begin with, the oaks were planted in a somewhat random fashion but over the last ten years, more trouble has been taken to visualise how they would look when mature, and in the newer planting areas sightlines have been left so that the visitor will be able to look through the oak plantings at the hills and features beyond. However, it is difficult to plan in detail as the trees grow at many different speeds and in many different shapes. This becomes doubly unpredictable with oaks which have not been grown in this country before.

From the start, it was decided to collect not only species but also hybrids and cultivars and in addition some *Lithocarpus*, which are closely related to oaks but are largely confined to the tropics. This implied a large number of individual trees. I have worked on the principle that many of the hybrids are better than their parents, and as we have the space, they should be tried. I try to plant two of each species and one of each hybrid but sometimes more have been planted for particular reasons. The sites vary in height from about 100 m to 200 m (328 to 656 ft), mostly south facing in deep slightly reddish loam, much of which is neutral but there are patches which are more acidic. Rainfall is around 86 cm (34 in) a year which is low by Devon standards but higher than in counties further east. Most oaks, including the desert ones, seem to cope with the rainfall although several of the white oaks grow very slowly while others grow exceptionally fast. Dr Owen Johnson, of the Tree Register, who visited the garden in the summer of 2007 found six Champion oak trees, including three Mexican species: *Quercus candicans*, *Q. affinis* and *Q. acherodophylla*, all of which have grown quickly and very straight. Some of the Chinese species have also grown remarkably fast, notably *Q. schottkyana*, as well as the Mexican *Q. sartorii*.

There have been some casualties along the way. We tend to lose one or two established trees each year either through wind or a poor root system sometimes aggravated by too much growth too quickly. About half

the oaks now flower with us but comparatively few yield viable acorns. This will improve as they mature and should produce some interesting hybrids. When young, the oaks have to cope with rabbits, squirrels, sheep, roe and red deer and the occasional caterpillar. Several oaks from semi-tropical areas, such as coastal Mexico and southern China have been planted. A few (for example, *Quercus insignis* and *Q. uxoris*) cannot take any frost and several others can suffer from frost damage, or perhaps more precisely, windchill, which can cut them back to ground level. If one can get a tree to grow to about 3 m with a reasonably thick bark, it has a good chance of surviving and, as we have had relatively warm winters for the last ten years, several marginal oaks seem to have become established.

The winter of 2008/9 was particularly difficult. First we had unusually hard frosts in October which affected the autumn growth of several of the species, then we had a very cold spell over Christmas and the New Year followed by a major snow storm on the night of February 5th. It started at 9pm and by the following morning there was over a foot of wet snow. There was also a high wind which caused a large accumulation of snow on many of the trees and particularly on the evergreen oaks. The result was that about fifteen of these trees suffered damage, ranging from being snapped off at the base in one case, to broken branches in others. However there was one minor miracle. We have one decent example of *Quercus crassipes*, which dates back to 1995 and is about 5 m (16 ft 4 in) high. It is perfectly shaped, with a 10 inch (25.4 cm) diameter trunk. In the February 2009 storm it was bent double with the upper branches frozen to the ground. The following morning I released these branches but the tree remained bent double. However, on the following day it had reverted to its upright position and does not seem to have suffered any permanent damage.

Building the collection

Early on we experimented in germinating acorns. This was under the expert guidance of Roy Gynn, a renowned gardener who knew the garden well and came, in retirement, to advise us at Chevithorne. He had green fingers and showed us how to germinate by hanging acorns in paper bags on the wall of the summer house, out of reach of the mice, in spring. We had surprisingly good results, which encouraged us to collect acorns from various unusual oaks taken from sites around the country.

Our system for germinating oaks has steadily become more sophisticated and we now have a very good success rate. More than half the collection has come from acorns we have germinated ourselves. These in turn have come from collectors, often based in England, who have been prepared to make trips to oak rich countries such as the wilder parts of China, Mexico and Japan.

Over the past ten years we have germinated a lot of seedlings of oaks collected all over the northern hemisphere, some rare, some not so rare. Obviously only one or two of each species find their way into our collection. This has thrown up a large number of spares which have been given to friends, acquaintances and visitors. I can count about forty different gardens in the UK where the oaks are now growing. They range from the north of Scotland to the tip of Cornwall, from West Wales to East Anglia and from sea level to 366 m (1,200 ft) in Perthshire. In general the success rate has been high, which helps to make the point that many of these introductions will grow satisfactorily anywhere in the UK. A small number have also been given to friends in Continental Europe, for example, Charles Fisher is growing *Quercus mexicana* near the Mediterranean coast, west of Montpellier, and Caroline Horsley is growing *Q. affinis* and *Q. fabri* near St Tropez.

The first oaks we bought came from Hillier Nurseries, soon followed by an introduction to James Harris of Mallet Court Nurseries (Curry Mallet, Somerset), who in those days was known as Acer Harris, but was in the process of switching the emphasis of his nursery to oaks. He has supplied us with many unusual oaks over the years, including two wonderful *Quercus candicans*, and he and his wife, Primrose, have been firm friends. We also used Burncoose Nurseries (Caerhays, Cornwall), Susan Cooper (Worcestershire) and Dulford Nurseries (Collompton, Devon) and later on, among others, Bluebell Nursery (Ashby de la Zouch, Leicestershire), Junkers Nursery (Taunton, Somerset) and Nick Macer of Pan-Global Plants (Frampton-on-Severn, Gloucestershire), who collects seeds for many of his own plants.

Quite early on I helped finance, for the first time, an expedition to look for seeds in the wild. One of the participants was Michael Hickson, at the time, the knowledgeable and influential Head Gardener at Knightshayes Court. His successor at Knightshayes, John Lanyon, who has now left that position, is also an excellent gardener with a profound knowledge of plants. The National Trust has recently decided to bring up to date their list of the vast array of plants and trees in the National Trust gardens. Some estimate that the combined collections of the National Trust properties are the biggest collection anywhere. The endangered plants will be reproduced at Knightshayes using various techniques, including hot grafting. As we are next door to Knightshayes, and helped by the family connection, we have built up a mutually satisfactory way of collaborating and co-operating to the advantage of both gardens. Michael Hickson went to Mexico in 1994 and came back with a good selection of acorns, not all of which had names, at least in the early stages, but several trees from this introduction are now over 12 m (39 ft) high, thus helping to prove the point that many Mexican oaks grow exceptionally well at Chevithorne Barton.

Around the same time we made contact with the Sir Harold Hillier Gardens and met for the first time Allen Coombes, who has, I believe, introduced more oaks into this country than anyone else. Allen possesses a great knowledge which he shares unselfishly and he, more than anyone, has had a seminal influence over our collection.

We have also been given unusual oaks or acorns by our friends and acquaintances, who had collected them, bought them, or sometimes found they had the wrong climate or garden for them and therefore could give them away. For example, John Ifold has given us a purple-leaved cork oak, which was a chance seedling from a packet of seeds obtained from Sheffield Seeds. It will be interesting to see if it stays purple as it grows as I do not think a purple cork oak has been recorded anywhere before. Those who have given us seedlings of unusual oaks include Ian Bond, Hugh Cavendish, Carol Gurney, Arabella Lennox-Boyd, Henk Maille, Eike Jablonski, Richard Storey, the late George Clive and the late Jo Earle. Those who have collected acorns for us in far away places include Shaun Haddock, the late Bill Legge-Bourke, Myles Bessborough, Dorothy Holley, Colin Chisholm and Jim Edwards to name a few. Other friends tried germinating spare acorns of ours using slightly different techniques and sometimes had success when we failed. For example, Alison De Ramsey at Abbots Ripton grew a good *Quercus polymorpha* from seed and gave the plant back to us.

In the early 1990s the International Oak Society was formed, bringing with it contact with oak enthusiasts all over the world. Several of them have helped us collect oaks, including Guy Sternberg, the Society's president in the early days, Eike Jablonski and Shaun Haddock, whose collection is in France and who personally found *Quercus baloot* in the mountains on the Afghanistan/Pakistan border. Then there were the continental nurseries, which in many cases have trees in their lists which are unobtainable commercially in the UK. Under this heading come Baumschule Döring (Ahnatal, Germany), Boomkwerkerij Pavia BVBA (Deerlijk, Belgium), Boomkerkerij M.M. Bömer (Zundert, The Netherlands), Pépinières Daniel Bastard (St-Philbert-en-Mauges, France), Firma C. Esveld (Boskoop, The Netherlands) and others. Sometimes the continental oaks are listed under a synonym which has caused temporary confusion, but almost invariably the continental plants are of good size and quality. There are two or three nurseries in Italy, such as Vannucci Piante, which specialise in larger trees: the only ones we have bought were to plant each side of our oak Millennium Bridge designed by Martin Lane Fox. They were about 5m (16 ft 4 in) high when planted, look remarkably well, but have hardly moved since we bought them, indicating that it is really not worthwhile buying large trees except perhaps to disguise an eyesore.

By no means least are the other collectors such as Michael Heseltine, who has an unparalleled and splendid collection of trees and shrubs at Thenford in Northamptonshire, of which oaks are only a small part. We have co-invested in seed hunting expeditions, swapped and given each other plants over the last fifteen years or so to our mutual advantage. Other collectors include the late Bill Legge-Bourke, Lloyd Kenyon, Tom Methuen-Campbell, Tom Hudson, and Christine Battle. All of them started collecting later than us but have brought energy, knowledge and enthusiasm to the oak world and all have built substantial and interesting collections. Christine, in addition, not only paints oaks quite beautifully (see page 6) but makes the time to organise the acorn hunting trips which seem to be becoming more numerous and successful every year. Then there is James MacEwen, who combines considerable erudition with a remarkable visual memory. He is also an excellent photographer and he has built up a collection of over a hundred species of seedling oaks in his minute London garden.

Most of the rarities and oaks which are difficult to establish have been acquired from specific expeditions, where the main purpose was to find the acorns of known species. Not everyone is capable of leading these expeditions, which are often to remote places and usually made in considerable discomfort. Here again Allen Coombes has been in the forefront, particularly in Mexico, often accompanied by his knowledgeable wife, Maricela. Further expedition leaders include Keith Rushforth in the Himalaya, Tony Kirkham in China, Beatrice Chassé in the United States, Shaun Haddock and Anke Mattern in Japan, and others. These journeys often led to acorns being collected, which eventually became trees that have not been grown in the UK before. Even if we know how these oaks behave in their natural habitat, they often grow differently in Devon, and at very different speeds. Tom Methuen-Campbell and Tom Hudson, one on the Gower Peninsula and the other on the south coast of Cornwall, have taken part in these expeditions either as leaders, participants or backers. They have virtually frost-free gardens, a definite advantage with oaks from the warmer parts of the world and, as a result, both have most interesting collections. Very recently, Henry Keswick gave us some acorns from an expedition he had sponsored to China's Dulong Valley (between Myanmar and Tibet).

The result of all this has been, and continues to be, a significant increase in the number of potentially available species of *Quercus* and *Lithocarpus* and their various hybrids and forms. Our collection has the scope and the space to increase considerably in the future. Global warming may help, as many introductions are on the borderline in terms of susceptibility to the English winter and especially spring frosts.

In summary we have tapped all available sources to build up the collection. As commercial sources run out, we increasingly rely on plant and seed collectors. However, there seems to be no lack of volunteers to go

to the wild, high and often inhospitable parts of the northern hemisphere, where the rare and obscure oaks tend to live: and then, of course, there is bureaucracy; more and more countries are protecting their natural environment and who can blame them. A modern seed collector has to know his way around the regulations of the country he is operating in. Often one needs a local partner and the ability to give something in return for taking away some acorns.

In March 1992 the collection was recognised by the National Council for the Conservation of Plants and Gardens (N.C.C.P.G.) – now known as Plant Heritage – and we were awarded National Collection® status, one of two such collections, the other being at the Sir Harold Hillier Gardens.

It is important that a National Collection® has proper records of its plants: in particular where the acorn or plant came from, whether it was wild collected, who collected it, the name under which it was received, and even what height it was growing at. From the start and until recently, Janet Richardson delt with this crucial part even though she lived over a hundred miles away. She also represented me at various International Oak Conferences and brought back valuable contacts and very often desirable acorns from the 'seed exchange' held at these conferences. She has played a vital and time-consuming role.

The oaks are usually planted in their final position when they are three or four years old. If they are planted in open ground where no trees or shrubs have grown in recent years we sprinkle in a handful of Rootgrow™. The beneficial bacteria and fungi in this seem to help the oak to keep growing, reducing the chance of a sulk, during which the tree hardly makes any progress, and which can last up to five years. We protect the trees as much as we can from the cold and some of the marginal oaks under 2 m (6 ft 7 in) are covered in netting for the three coldest months of the year. Not all species produce elegant upright trees and on some we leave the low branches. Over the years the oaks have required pruning and shaping. Most look better as a tree than as a shrub, but there are exceptions. *Quercus pontica*, for example, looks better as a shrub with multiple stems, and others, for example, *Q. monimotricha*, develop naturally into a low mound. I believe it to be true that the more experienced you are, the less mercy you show as a pruner. Certainly the most ruthless pruners who have been allowed near our trees are Tony Kirkham of Kew and Michael Hickson, who have much expertise and experience. Both are capable of pruning 60% of the branches off a tree in one go and one has to admit that the tree invariably looks better for its haircut the following year. We tend to be more cautious and would not normally prune more than 25% of the branches in one go but we may prune a tree many times before we are satisfied with the shape.

The collection now

By the beginning of February 2009, we had 382 differently named oaks in the collection. This included 225 species, subspecies and varieties, and 157 other forms, made up of 58 hybrids and 99 cultivars such as variegated and purple-leaved versions of a species. This is against a background of perhaps 500 known species. Geographically, and bearing in mind that *Quercus* come from all over the northern hemisphere (with the exception of one or two oaks from Borneo and one from Colombia and Panama) our European coverage is fairly comprehensive as is our collection of oaks from the Near East, which includes Turkey and the Caucasus.

In the Far East, where there is a large number of oaks, we have fair representation from the more northerly parts such as Japan, Korea, the Himalaya and Northern China, but much less representation from the hotter regions and almost no representation from Indo-China and Borneo. Further, it is fair to say that most of the oaks in these areas could not tolerate our climate, except in the greenhouse.

We have fairly good representation from the United States, where there are around 90 species of oaks. We also have about 75 Mexican oaks, if one includes naturally occurring hybrids and oaks that are also found in the south of the United States. There are more different species of oaks in Mexico than in any other country. No one knows exactly how many, but there are certainly 160, and probably more like 200, as the country has not been comprehensively searched. It is significant that Allen Coombes collected two new species during his recent expedition to Mexico. We have recently obtained *Quercus humboldtii*, whose natural distribution is Panama and Colombia. I believe it to be true that we have more Mexican oaks at Chevithorne than there are in any single collection in Mexico.

South of Mexico, going towards the Equator, we also have a few species from the mountain regions of Honduras and Guatemala.

We also have three oaks which from experience we have to keep in the greenhouse in the winter. They are *Quercus cubana* (Cuba never has a frost), *Q. insignis* and *Q. uxoris* from the semi-tropical rain forests of Mexico.

The genus *Lithocarpus* is closely related to *Quercus* and considered by many people to be covered by the name oak. *Lithocarpus* mostly come from the hotter parts of East and South East Asia except for one rather distinct species which comes from southern Oregon and California. We have a small collection of several different species mostly from China and Taiwan. Two of them have been growing satisfactorily at Chevithorne for ten years or so but the others have only been planted out in their final positions for the past three years. In spite of finding the winters rather cold they are looking remarkably well. Several of them have grown at an above average speed and look as if they will make good trees in due course.

The future

From the outset, I intended the collection to be as comprehensive a collection of oaks as our climate allowed, bearing in mind that although we live in Devon, Chevithorne Barton is over 25 miles from both the north and south coasts and around 150 m (492 ft) above sea level. It is rather damp by southern England standards (rainfall is about 35 in / 88.9 cm a year). We also get our share of snow and a fair number of early and late frosts. The latter can be mitigated against by careful planting but in most years they do affect quite a number of oaks, many of which tend to put on growth early in the spring or late in the autumn and are therefore more susceptible to subsequent cold winters.

At present many of the oaks are still small, but in fifty years time, the garden and surrounding landscape at Chevithorne will have changed profoundly. My grandmother's plantswoman's garden will have evolved and be framed in the context of a landscape dominated by mature oak trees. Our oaks grow at different speeds, sometimes faster and sometimes slower than in their countries of origin. A traditional English oak will still take more than a hundred years to reach maturity, but some of the American oaks will be mature in less than fifty. A few of the Mexican oaks are currently growing as fast as bamboos – between 1 and 2 m (3 ft 6 in to 7 ft 2 in) a year, but for how long we do not know, and it may leave them weak and unable to withstand the strong winds that seem to be becoming more frequent.

When they are young, the trees benefit from being planted relatively close together for shelter, although they need full sunlight as well. Several have had to be moved from sheltered to sunnier positions. As they grow older, some will have to be thinned out to ensure that the remainder have room to reach their full potential. So, wherever possible, we like to have several specimens, especially of rarer and more vulnerable trees.

Several decades after embarking modestly on our oak project, I feel that in some ways we are still just starting out. There is much more to do, both in looking after the oaks that we already have to give them the best chance to thrive, and in expanding the collection to the limits of what will grow here. And we have come to be grateful that we are in Devon because the combination of relatively warm winters, reasonably high rainfall, and strong, deep, loamy soil seems to suit nearly all the oaks we are trying to grow. In other words the range of oaks we are growing is unusually diverse. Climate change may well play a part in setting our parameters, although whether that means warmer weather, or merely more variable and extreme conditions, remains to be seen. Whatever happens, I hope Chevithorne's oak collection remains very much a work in progress for many years to come.

right: *Q. suber* at Antony House in Cornwall (a National Trust property)

The propagation of oaks

By James MacEwen, FLS
Fulham, London, UK

When possible our oaks are propagated from seed collected from wild sources. The necessity of this is that they easily hybridise and rarely grow true from acorns collected from gardens. Even in wild-collected seed, natural hybrids may occur.

If the seed collected is healthy, acorns usually germinate easily, although we all, of course, have failures. At Chevithorne Barton, David Lancelles, the Head Gardener grows the acorns in Rootrainers®. He uses a mix of three parts compost to one part grit. The compost used is multi-purpose with Sincro-Boost (a natural product derived from recycled organic materials). The grit is a coarse grit, washed, lime free and of horticultural grade. At the Sir Harold Hillier Gardens, Barry Clarke, who is the propagator and nursery manager, similarly works with Rootrainers®. He uses a peat-free soil mix made from compost bark, perlite for drainage and vermiculite for some moisture retention.

Acorns are placed on their sides and pressed into the soil so that 50% of the seed is above the surface. A fine layer of Cornish grit is then put on top of the seed: this allows for effective drainage but some moisture retention. Acorns are prone to rot if buried too deeply in sodden soil. Pests can be a problem and both squirrels and mice raid growing areas which are not secure. At Chevithorne Barton a wire cover is placed over the Rootrainers®. Protection is equally needed against other pests such as slugs, snails etc. In cool conditions, acorns tend to germinate around February, March and April, although some species have been found to germinate in the second season – *Lithocarpus edulis* for example.

Other forms of propagation have been used successfully and certain species of evergreen oaks can be grown from cuttings. *Quercus acuta* grows particularly easily but *Q. semecarpifolia*, *Q. insignis* and *Q. rysophylla* have also been rooted by Tom Hudson at Tregrehan. Cuttings can take a year to eighteen months to form roots. At Congrove, Christine Battle's best success has been achieved by taking semi-hardwood cuttings in early July. She places the cuttings round the edge of a shallow pot with four or five cuttings per pot. The cuttings are around 15–20 cm long and submerged by 2/3 of their length, their bases having been dipped in hormone rooting powder. All but three leaves are removed and, if large, about 2/3 of each remaining leaf is cut off. The pots are then watered, well sprayed with an anti-fungicide and placed inside a plastic bag, which has also been similarly sprayed. The bag is secured, placed on a heated bench and checked regularly to remove any cuttings that may have rotted. As soon as there is a sign of growth the cuttings are removed from the heat bench. At the Sir Harold Hillier Gardens, the best method they found for rooting evergreen cuttings was using mist with under-bench heating.

Oaks can also be grafted, and Barry Clarke has successfully grafted several *Q. robur* cultivars on to the species using both side-veneer and budding grafting techniques. Red oaks are grafted on red oak stock and white oaks likewise on white oaks.

At Chevithorne the young trees are transplanted from Rootrainers® into successive pots until they reach a height of 30–90 cm (1–3 ft). The young trees are very prone to attack by deer and badgers so suitable safeguards are needed. Tony Kirkham, Head of the Arboretum at Kew, is very insistent that trees should not be planted in round holes as the roots have a habit of following the edges of the dug holes and when doing this with a round hole, they form root balls, whereas if the roots find a corner they will force their way through it searching for fresh soil. The stem of the plant should be at the same soil level as it was in the pot or ground that it came from on re-planting and great care should be taken to ensure it is not below this level. Introduction of mycorrhizal fungi to aid root growth is becoming more common and is certainly considered worthwhile. If the planting is in ground which has not had trees or shrubs on it recently, the mycorrhiza seems to stop some oaks from sulking when they are moved. Proprietary products containing mycorrhizal fungi, such as Rootgrow™, which is in pellet form, are becoming widely available. Staking should be done as necessary.

In summary, oaks can be reproduced from seed, by grafting and, exceptionally, by taking cuttings. All three options have advantages and disadvantages. The disadvantage of germination is that one cannot be sure the acorn has not hybridised. Grafting sometimes leads to trouble when the trees are fully grown in that the graft can be a weak spot prone to breaking at the join. Cuttings take with difficulty and those that do tend to be from evergreen species.

The origins of oaks

By Professor Richard Jensen
St Mary's College, Notre Dame,
Indiana, USA

The oaks (Family Fagaceae, genus *Quercus*) belong to an old lineage of trees and shrubs that dates back to at least the Late Cretaceous (about 85 million years ago). The oldest fossils are most closely aligned with *Fagus*, the beeches, but there are also suggestions of chestnuts (*Castanea*) in some of these ancient materials. These fossils are known, to date, only from Georgia in the south eastern United States. When it comes to the origin of the oaks (*Quercus* spp.), there is much better evidence. The fossil record reveals that trees similar to oaks first appear about 32-35 million years ago, and trees related to extant species appear by about 25 million years ago. By about 23 million years ago, trees representative of most major groups of oaks have appeared.

Oaks are characterised by their fruits – acorns. In botanical terms, the acorn consists of two components: a nut and a cupule. The nut is derived from the ovary of a female flower. The cupule is derived from a series of scales, or bracts, that are found at the base of the female flower. Both the cupule and the nut have distinctive features that allow us to readily identify trees that belong to *Quercus*. However, there is another group of plants in Fagaceae that also produce acorns, or acorn-like fruits. The stone oaks (genus *Lithocarpus*) are native to South East Asia, with one species, *Lithocarpus densiflorus* (the tan oak) occurring in the western United States. Interestingly, the acorn of the stone oaks appears to be analogous to, not homologous with, the acorn of *Quercus*. That is, despite their superficial similarities, these acorns have separate evolutionary origins.

Taxonomists have dealt with the morphological diversity of acorn-bearing plants in a variety of ways. Historically, all acorn-bearing plants were classified in the genus *Quercus*, the classical Latin name for oak. This practice was followed, more or less uniformly, until the late 1800s. By that time, several botanists had recognised that the stone oaks, usually identified as a subgenus or section of *Quercus*, comprised a separate genus, *Lithocarpus* (=*Pasania*). Despite the acknowledgement that the stone oaks represent a separate genus, the so-called 'true oaks' remain a quite diverse assemblage of plants. Most of us recognise the more-or-less typical lobed leaves of English oak (*Q. robur*), white oak (*Q. alba*), northern red oak (*Q. rubra*) and black oak (*Q. velutina*). However, for many of us the toothed leaves of cork oak (*Q. suber*), chestnut oak (*Q. montana*) or sawtooth oak (*Q. acutissima*) seem a little strange and the entire leaves of shingle oak (*Q. imbricaria*), willow oak (*Q. phellos*) and interior live oak (*Q. wislizeni*) are simply odd for an oak.

Because of the great diversity of leaf form, as well as clear differences in cupule features, the oaks have been divided into many taxonomic groups. As a prelude to this, the reader needs to know that, in the taxonomic hierarchy, *Quercus* is a genus. The species within a genus may be divided into additional groups based on a variety of characteristics. Typically, a genus may be divided into two or more subgenera and a subgenus may be divided into groups referred to as sections. If there are distinctly different groups among the species of a section, these may be organised into smaller sets called series. The oaks in *Quercus* have been organised into all of these taxonomic categories by the various botanists who have studied them and tried to classify them.

top: young growth on *Q. kellogii*
above: *Q. guajavifolia*

Thus, species that are very similar may be grouped into a series, similar series will belong to the same section, and two or more sections may belong to a single subgenus.

A classic example of such a classification may be seen in William Trelease's taxonomy of the American oaks published in the mid 1920s. Trelease recognised three subgenera of *Quercus* in the New World, *Leucobalanus* (the white and chestnut oaks), *Erythrobalanus* (the red and black oaks) and *Protobalanus* (the intermediate oaks), as well as three additional subgenera for the oaks of the Old World: *Cerris*, *Cyclobalanopsis* and *Heterobalanus*. Although he did not recognise sections within each subgenus, Trelease did divide the American oaks into over 150 series, most consisting of only one or two morphologically quite similar species.

Some of the groups Trelease recognised were a reflection of earlier classifications. One of the more important was that of Anders Oersted, a Danish botanist who, in 1867, recognised five subgenera in *Quercus*. At the same time, Oersted also created a new genus, *Cyclobalanopsis*, for those cycle-cup (the cup scales, instead of overlapping as do roof shingles, form concentric rings around the central axis) oaks that were most closely related to the true oaks. The French botanist Aimée Camus was the last person to try to classify the oaks on a worldwide basis. In her monograph (published during the 1930s), she recognised two subgenera of oaks, *Cyclobalanopsis* and *Euquercus*, the latter being divided into six sections: *Cerris*, *Mesobalanus*, *Lepidobalanus* (= Trelease's *Leucobalanus* in part), *Macrobalanus*, *Protobalanus* and *Erythrobalanus*.

More recently, Kevin Nixon (Cornell University) conducted careful studies to evaluate the status of these taxonomic groups as well as the correct taxonomic names for each. Nixon concluded that *Quercus* consists of two subgenera, *Quercus* (= Camus's *Euquercus*) and *Cyclobalanopsis*. Further, *Quercus* subgenus *Quercus* was divided into four sections: *Quercus*, *Lobatae*, *Protobalanus* and *Cerris*. Nixon's classification has been accepted by most students of *Quercus*. However, in their recent taxonomic treatments of Fagaceae in the *Flora of China* and the *Flora Reipublicae Popularis Sinicae*, C.C. Chang and colleagues have followed Oersted's classification by treating *Cyclobalanopsis* as a genus.

The advent of modern molecular biology has provided valuable insights into plant relationships and Paul Manos (a student of Nixon) and his students have drawn some very important conclusions from their studies of DNA patterns among the Fagaceae. These studies (Paul Manos, Alice Stanford, Charles Cannon and Sang-Hun Oh) have revealed that, in an evolutionary sense, the stone oaks and the true oaks are, indeed, separate groups and their classification into different genera is well justified. What may be more interesting for those of us familiar with the true oaks is that the two primary groups of oaks recognised by Camus and Nixon (although given different names, Camus's subgenus *Euquercus* and Nixon's subgenus *Quercus* include the same species of *Quercus*) turn out not to be good taxonomic groups. Specifically, Manos and his students have shown that section *Cerris* should not be included in subgenus *Quercus*. Rather, the true oaks are divided into two primary groups: one group consisting of the traditional subgenus *Cyclobalanopsis* together with section *Cerris*; the other group comprising the remaining species. Thus, this molecular work suggests that *Cyclobalanopsis* is not a separate genus and that *Quercus* subgenus *Quercus* is not a monophyletic group.

This latest finding has yet to be reflected in nomenclatural changes. However, it shows that the evolution of the true oaks is a fascinating and complex story. As we continue to learn about these most important trees, there will certainly be additional changes to the current taxonomic classification. Do not be surprised if our view of what is really an oak undergoes some significant changes in the near future.

Cladogram of Fagaceae

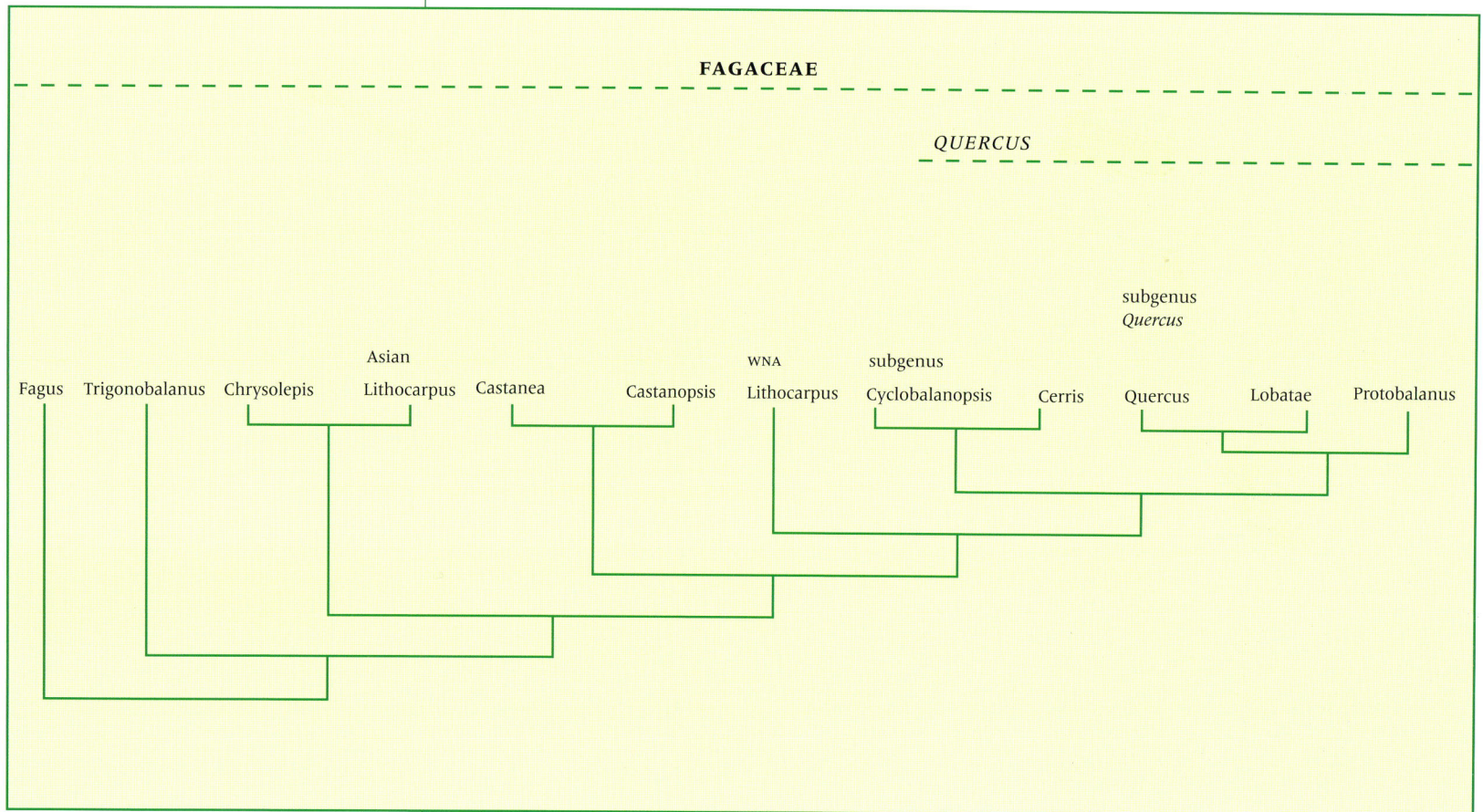

right: A developing cupule on
Q. macrolepis 'Hemelrijk Silver'

The classification of oaks

By Allen Coombes
Botanist at the Sir Harold Hillier Gardens,
Hampshire, UK

The oaks are a genus of some 450–500 species of deciduous and evergreen trees and shrubs. They are widely distributed across the northern hemisphere but absent from the colder areas of the far north, and extend south to Colombia in South America and Indonesia, where they just enter the southern hemisphere. Oaks definitely prefer warm climates and the greatest diversity of species occurs in warm temperate, subtropical and tropical regions. The further south an oak grows, the more likely it is to be restricted to mountain regions.

Within the genus, the species are extremely varied, ranging from large trees of 40 m (130 ft) or more to small, sometimes suckering shrubs of 1 m or less. While most will identify an oak from its leaf, this is perhaps the most variable aspect, ranging from large with rounded or pointed lobes, to saw-toothed, spiny or entire (without lobes or teeth). What does remain constant is that they all have separate male and female flowers, the males in pendulous catkins (thus distinguishing them from *Castanea* and *Lithocarpus*). All have an acorn for the fruit which can vary a great deal in size and shape, as can the scaly cup in which it is borne.

The genus is divided into two major groups, or subgenera. Most of the familiar species are in subgenus *Quercus*. The other group, subgenus *Cyclobalanopsis*, is still treated by some as a genus in its own right but, as Professor Jensen has pointed out in this book, current molecular work confirms its placement within the genus *Quercus*. Members of subgenus *Cyclobalanopsis*, sometimes referred to as the ring-cup oaks, are restricted to Asia, occurring from the western Himalaya in Pakistan to East and South East Asia. They are evergreen, or sometimes briefly deciduous, trees and shrubs with entire or shallowly toothed leaved. The scales on the acorn cup are united into concentric rings. There about 150 species, many in tropical and subtropical regions. The most familiar species in gardens are *Q. glauca* and *Q. myrsinifolia*.

Subgenus *Quercus*, which contains the remainder of the species, is further subdivided into sections. Section *Quercus*, the white oaks, consists of deciduous and evergreen trees and shrubs widely distributed in North and Central America, Europe, North Africa and Asia. They normally have leaves with rounded lobes or with short, blunt teeth, occasionally entire. The acorns ripen in the first year (and so are found on the shoot amongst the leaves) and germinate as soon as they fall. Examples of this section are English oak (*Q. robur*) and white oak (*Q. alba*).

Section *Lobatae*, the red oaks, also consists of deciduous and evergreen trees and shrubs but these are confined to North and Central America. While there are more technical differences between these and the white oaks, they often have leaves with pointed lobes ending in bristle-like teeth. The acorns usually ripen in the second year (and so are found on mature, leafless shoots) and they normally germinate during the following year. Well-known examples of this section are red oak (*Q. rubra*) and pin oak (*Q. palustris*).

Section *Cerris* consists of evergreen and deciduous trees and shrubs found only in Europe, North Africa and Asia. These oaks often have conspicuous stipules, their acorns normally ripen in the second year, and the cups often have bristly scales. Although these oaks have often been included in section *Quercus*, Professor Jensen points out that recent work shows that they are in fact very distinct and are more closely related to the oaks of subgenus *Cyclobalanopsis* than to the other oaks. Examples of this section are Turkey oak (*Q. cerris*) and sawtooth oak (*Q. acutissima*).

Section *Protobalanus*, the intermediate oaks, consists of only five species of evergreen trees and shrubs from the south west United States and north west Mexico. They have leathery leaves with spiny teeth, at least when juvenile, and acorns that ripen in the second year. The best known species is golden cup oak (*Q. chrysolepis*).

Hybridisation between different species in the genus, both in the wild and in cultivation, broadly confirms these divisions. Hybrids within subgenus *Cyclobalanopsis* are reported from Japan but no hybrids have been found between any member of this subgenus and subgenus *Quercus*. Members of section *Quercus* and section *Lobatae* hybridise very frequently, both in the wild and in cultivation, but only within their sections. No hybrids are known between these sections. Some are known in section *Protobalanus* but only within that section. Curiously, it is section *Cerris* that is the odd one out here. Certainly, hybrids are known within this section but only one hybrid with a member of section *Lobatae* is known: *Q. ×kewensis* (*Q. cerris* × *Q. wislizeni*), and a small number of hybrids also occur with members of section *Quercus*, such as *Q. ×turneri* (*Q. ilex* × *Q. robur*).

Q. castaneifolia at Kew Gardens

Quercus acherdophylla Trel.

Mexico

A vigorous tree growing 15 m or more in the wild and proving very hardy in cultivation. Shoots glabrous, leaves short-stalked, elliptic-oblong to oblanceolate, wavy-edged and untoothed except for a short point at the tip, to 10 × 3.5 cm. Bronze and hairy when young they become bright glossy green and glabrous above, glabrous or thinly hairy beneath with small tufts of hairs in the vein axils. Acorns ovoid to nearly spherical, ripening the first year, about 1 cm long, borne singly or in pairs on a short stalk.

Introduced to cultivation by Michael Frankis of Northumberland in 1991: collection unnamed.

This oak thrives at Chevithorne Barton. There are five specimens planted in a variety of sites, some sheltered, some exposed to the prevailing wind, some damp, some comparatively dry. All have grown astonishingly fast with a good upright habit. The tallest is already 12 m high, making it the UK Champion Tree. The trees are all very hardy and evergreen but no acorns have been seen yet. There are no reasons why this tree cannot be grown virtually anywhere in the UK.

Quercus acuta Thunb.

Japan, S Korea

An evergreen tree that can reach a large size in the wild, this species is slow-growing in cultivation and usually makes a small bushy tree. The long-stalked, oval, leathery leaves are untoothed or with a few small teeth, up to 12 cm long and ending in a long, tapered point. Green on both sides when mature, they are very attractive when they open, being covered in silky hairs. The acorns ripen the first year and are borne in short spikes in downy cups. The foliage is somewhat similar to that of *Lithocarpus edulis* and the two are occasionally confused in gardens. It has been distributed as *Q. cuspidata*, a synonym of *Castanopsis cuspidata*.

First introduced to Europe in 1877 by Charles Maries of Caerhays, Gorran, Cornwall, where it has reached 14 m.

There are three specimens at Chevithorne Barton, the tallest being 3 m high. Although a slow grower, it makes a neat small tree which is hardy. At first glance it is rather difficult to see that it is an oak.

Subgenus *Cyclobalanopsis*

C & S Mexico, C America

In its native Mexico, this species can reach more than 30 m, and usually loses its leaves in late winter when they turn yellow. The lance-shaped leaves are up to 15 cm long, or more, with seven–ten bristle-tipped teeth on each side and with a taper-pointed tip. Glossy dark green above when mature and glabrous or nearly so on both sides, they are often bronze or red when young. The acorns are about 1.5 cm long in a hemispherical cup and ripen the second year. It forms hybrids with *Q. mexicana*, where the two species grow together.

Introduced to cultivation by Allen Coombes from Puebla, Mexico in 1995.

This is another oak that grows vigorously and fast at Chevithorne Barton. There are four specimens, the tallest has reached 7 m in twelve years, and the other ones are not far behind. It appears to be completely hardy in Devon.

Quercus acutissima Carruth.

Sawtooth oak
China, Japan, Korea

A vigorous, deciduous tree that can attain a large size. The oblong, chestnut-like leaves to 20 cm long bear numerous parallel veins that end in slender, bristle-tipped teeth. They are bright glossy green above, pale beneath, and turn yellow-brown in autumn. Acorns are rarely seen in this country. They are 2–2.5 cm long, borne in a cup covered with recurved hairy scales and ripen the second year.

Introduced by Richard Oldham, gardener at Kew, in about 1862. It has reached 20 m at Lytchett Heath, Dorset.

There are two good specimens at Chevithorne Barton, one of which, planted in 1986 between the swimming pool and tennis court, is a handsome tree 19 m tall that looks set to grow a lot taller. Both appear to be completely hardy and could be grown anywhere in the southern counties.

Q. chenii Nakai (*Q. acutissima* subsp. *chenii* (Nakai) A. Camus). This Chinese species is very close to *Q. acutissima* but differs in its smaller acorns and cups. Plants in cultivation also have shorter and narrower leaves and are slower growing. It has reached 10 m tall at the Hillier Gardens. There are three specimens of this tree here. They are smaller – the biggest is about 4 m tall, more delicate, and less upright than *Q. acutissima*.

left, centre: *Q. acutissima*
bottom right, top right: *Q. chenii*

Quercus affinis Scheidw.

Mexico

A vigorous and hardy evergreen tree that can reach 30 m in its native habitat where it is found in the mountains at high altitudes. The lance-shaped leaves, to about 10 cm long and 3 cm wide, are glossy green and smooth above, paler beneath with conspicuous tufts of hair in the vein axils. Variable in shape, they usually have three–four bristle-tipped teeth on each side, but on some forms leaves are entire. The acorns ripen the second year and are about 1.5 cm long in a hemispherical cup about 1 cm across, borne singly or in pairs on a short stalk. The upright habit, fast growth and often coppery to bronze young foliage make this a handsome species.

Introduced by Jim Priest of Kew in 1984.

There are five good specimens at Chevithorne Barton. All are growing well with excellent shapes. Unusually for a Mexican oak, they are completely hardy even in the open. The tallest, at 11 m, was measured by Dr Owen Johnson, Assistant Registrar for the Tree Register in 2007 and pronounced the UK Champion Tree (although apparently there is a taller one at Kew). The other four plants seem likely to grow even taller. In mid-December 2007 there was no sign of leaf drop.

Q. laurina Humb. & Bonpl. is a Mexican species closely related to *Q. affinis*, and intermediates occur. It can usually be distinguished by the leaves that are untoothed towards the base and broadest above the middle. These are upright trees of narrow habit, whose most striking characteristic is the bark, often described as pachydermatous. This oak seems to be hardy, except for some possible damage to the bark in cold winters. Leaves in mid-December show no sign of dropping or turning. There are four of these trees here, the tallest 7 m.

left, centre: *Q. affinis*
top right, bottom right: *Q. laurina*

Quercus agrifolia Née

California live oak, Coast live oak
California, Mexico (Baja California)

This hardy evergreen species can reach 25 m
in California, where it occurs on slopes and
in canyons in the coastal ranges. It can be
recognised by its distinctly convex leaves,
which are oval and up to 7 cm long. They are
glossy dark green and smooth above, paler
and hairy, at least in the vein axils beneath,
and can be edged with either spiny teeth or
smooth margins. The acorns ripen the first
year and are conical to 3.5 cm long.

Introduced by Carl Hartweg, collector for
the Royal Horticultural Gardens in 1849, it has
reached 17 m at Exbury Gardens, Hampshire.

There are four specimens of these oaks at
Chevithorne Barton, where they grow fast
with dense foliage. The tallest is around 9 m.
This oak is evergreen and completely hardy
in Devon. The best tree here was spoilt by
the spring storm in 2007, which shattered
half its branches.

Golden oak of Cyprus
Cyprus

This very distinct evergreen, making a large shrub or small tree about 5–8 m tall, is only found in the Troodos mountains of Cyprus. The rigid, leathery, rounded to broadly oval leaves are up to 6 cm long. They are glossy dark green above with distinctly impressed veins and covered beneath with a golden felt, at least when young. The acorns are up to 4 cm long and widen noticeably above the base. They ripen the first year and are borne in a short cup densely covered in bristly scales. Unusually for oaks, the acorns germinate from the base. It is a slow-growing but hardy species, which has a restricted distribution and is listed as Vulnerable in the Red List of Oaks.

Introduced to Kew in 1885. It has reached 8 m at East Bergholt Place, Suffolk.

There are three specimens at Chevithorne Barton. The first to be planted is in a sheltered but rather shady position east of the walled garden. It has been growing there for ten years but is still only 0.5 m tall, yet appears healthy with new growth each year. The second planting is in the rockery and set to grow slightly faster. This is the only golden oak outside of the Far East where there are several species, mainly in China.

Quercus argyrotricha A. Camus

S China

A spreading evergreen tree related to *Q. oxyodon* and growing to 10 m or more, the young shoots covered in yellowish hairs becoming more or less smooth with age. Leaves elliptic to oblong, to 12 cm long and 5 cm across, ending in a tapered point and prominently marked with up to fourteen veins on each side that end in sharp teeth. They are an attractive bronze when young, becoming glossy green above with yellowish white hairs below. Acorns broadly ovoid to 1.5 cm long, hairy when young, ripening the second year and borne on a very short stalk, the cup covered in yellow hairs and with seven–nine rings.

This rare species was introduced from Yunnan, China, in 2004 by Allen Coombes, who found it with Prof. Zhekun Zhou, Kunming, China. Prior to this it was only known from one site in Guizhou. It is listed as Endangered in the Red List of Oaks.

We have two young plants of this species at Chevithorne Barton. It has exceptionally attractive leaves, grows vigorously, and if it can adapt to our climate, has the possibility of being a really worthwhile introduction. The two plants growing outside survived their first winter successfully.

Q. pentacycla Y.T. Chang is closely related to *Q. argyrotricha* but has smooth shoots and larger leaves to 14 cm long. The acorn cup is covered in whitish hairs and has four–five rings. Introduced from Yunnan by Allen Coombes in 1998, it has grown well here to more than 2 m tall and has attractive red young foliage.

top left, bottom left: *Q. argyrotricha*
top centre, bottom centre, right: *Q. pentacycla*

Arkansas oak
SE United States (Florida to Texas)

A deciduous tree growing to about 15 m or, occasionally, to 25 m in its native habitats, where it can usually be found on sandy or rocky soils. The obovate leaves up to 10 cm long are unlobed to shallowly lobed, narrowed to the base and edged with few small, bristle-like teeth. Leaves on the second flush of growth are usually more distinctly lobed. Covered with hairs as they emerge, they eventually become more or less smooth except for tufts of hairs in the axils of the veins. The rounded acorns ripen the second year and are borne in a shallow cup. Some leaves can resemble those of the Blackjack oak (*Q. marilandica*), which has thicker leaves with yellowish hairs beneath. Listed as Vulnerable in the Red List of Oaks. It has reached 14 m at Kew.

There are two established specimens at Chevithorne Barton, the tallest about 7 m in height. A neat, good-looking tree which grows slowly in Devon and usually has good autumn colour.

Quercus baloot Griff.

W Himalaya (N Pakistan, Afghanistan, Kashmir)

An evergreen tree or shrub to 12 m with dark grey bark divided into rectangular plates. Branchlets grey tomentose to brown and glabrous. Leaves to about 5 cm long, obovate or elliptic or, rarely, circular, leathery, with the upper surface greyish-green, lower surface white or glaucous with stellate tomentum. Leaves on mature trees can have sharply spiny or entire margins, while seedlings from both have spiny margins. The acorns are elliptic and ripen the first year. It is closely related to *Q. ilex* and strongly resembles plants of the Iberian *Q. rotundifolia*.

The plant inhabits the dry valleys of the Himalaya and Hindu Kush between 1,800 and 3,000 m, and is adapted to drought and extremes of heat and cold. It is therefore not a vigorous species. Surprisingly rare in cultivation considering its origin, it was introduced by Shaun Haddock, France, from acorns he collected in the Swat Valley, North-West Frontier Province of Pakistan, in October 1995.

A specimen at Hillier Gardens from this collection has attained a height of 2.6 m.

We have one small plant from Shaun's original collection, which was first planted out in 2001 in a rather exposed position. It was unhealthy and suffered considerable dieback. In 2003 it was replanted in a sheltered, dry, protected site where it produces healthy new growth and is currently 1 m tall and growing vigorously.

Swamp white oak
E United States, SE Canada

A large, spreading deciduous tree in the wild with flaking bark, this species can reach 25–30 m tall or more and is found in lowland, often swampy areas. In Britain, it performs better than most of the other American white oaks, which often suffer from lack of summer heat to ripen the wood. The large, obovate leaves to 15 cm or more long are narrowed to the base and edged with shallow lobes. They are glossy dark green above and covered with white hairs beneath, turning yellow or red in autumn. The large, sweet acorns to 2.5 cm long ripen the first year and are borne, often in pairs, on a long stalk. However, they are rarely produced in this country.

Introduced in 1800, it has reached 22 m at Kew.

At Chevithorne Barton there is one established tree which was slow to get going but is now about 4.5 m tall and seems to be perfectly happy in our climate. By mid-December, half the leaves have fallen off.

Q. lyrata Walter (Overcup oak). This large deciduous tree of the Southeastern United States is related to *Q. bicolor* but has deeply lobed leaves, green on both sides. The acorns are very distinct in being almost or completely enclosed in the cup. This species requires hot summers to thrive and is not generally successful in this country. Two specimens here planted in the early 1990s are decently shaped small trees, the tallest about 6 m. This is quite satisfactory for a white oak but they are unlikely to reach anything like the size they grow to in their natural habitat.

Q. michauxii Nutt. (Swamp chestnut oak, Basket oak). Another species from the Southeastern United States, this large tree of moist and swampy areas generally needs more summer heat than we can provide to grow well. It has large obovate leaves edged with numerous shallow lobes and large acorns on short stalks. The two trees here have struggled with frost damage and cool summers but one seems to be established and is now 3 m in height.

Q. oglethorpensis W.H. Duncan. The Oglethorpe oak is a rare species from the Southeastern United States. It has entire elliptic to oblanceolate leaves, toothed on the second flush, which resemble those of the red oak, *Q. imbricaria*. Introduced to the Hillier Gardens in 1978, where it has reached 9 m. It is listed as Endangered in the Red List of Oaks. There are two young trees here, the tallest about 1 m tall.

Q. ×warei T.L. Green & W.J. Hess. This hybrid between *Q. bicolor* and *Q. robur* (mainly Fastigiata Group) has occurred several times in the United States and there are now several cultivars available that promise to make attractive trees of upright habit. There is one small plant of this at Chevithorne Barton and a better one of *Q. ×warei* 'Windcandle' (*Q. bicolor* × *Q. robur* Fastigiata Group) which was selected by Guy Sternberg of the Starhill Forest Arboretum, Illinois, USA. It was planted here in 2005 and looks promising at 1.5 m.

top left: *Q. oglethorpensis*
bottom left: *Q. lyrata*
right: *Q. bicolor*

Quercus canariensis Willd.

Algerian oak
S Spain, S Portugal, N Africa

This magnificent tree sometimes reaches more than 30 m and is one of the finest large oaks grown in this country. It is semi-evergreen, usually remaining in leaf until well into winter or early spring. The bold obovate leaves are up to 20 cm or more and edged with numerous shallow lobes. Hairy on both side at first, they become glossy dark green above and blue-green beneath. The hairs on the underside of the leaf rub off easily but the few tufts that remain in the leaf axils and along the midrib help to identify this species. The acorns are 3–4 cm long and ripen the first year. They are unstalked or on short stalks and borne clustered on the shoots in downy cups.

This species has often been raised from garden seed and trees can be found in many collections that are hybrids with *Q. robur* (= *Q. ×carrissoana*) or *Q. petraea* (= *Q. ×viveri*).

Introduced in about 1854, it has reached 30 m at Tregrehan, St Austell, Cornwall.

It grows well at Chevithorne Barton where we have a fine young tree 5.5 m high, planted in 2002. An older, bigger specimen is a hybrid but we also have a smaller leaved form which is sometimes called *Q. mirbeckii*, and which is one of the oaks that can be recommended for planting in a park-like landscape.

NE Mexico

Of relatively recent introduction, this vigorous semi-evergreen tree of spreading habit is proving hardy. It grows in forests on mountain slopes in the wild and is often found in association with *Q. rysophylla*. The glossy dark green leaves, often bronze when young, are up to 12 cm long and edged with four–five bristle-tipped lobes. Hairy on both sides when young, they become almost glabrous except for tufts of hair in the vein axils on the underside. Unusually for oaks of this sort, the acorns ripen in the first year. They are up to 1.5 cm long, sometimes much shorter, and are borne singly or in small clusters on a short stalk.

Introduced by Sir Harold Hillier in 1979, it has reached 15 m at the Hillier Gardens.

At Chevithorne Barton we have two recently planted trees and one which has been in for ten years, and although it has only grown to 3.5 m in that time, it is a perfectly shaped small tree with attractive leaves, and is perfectly hardy. One of the more recently planted trees is already 4 m tall. In January 2008 it had shiny green leaves: rare and attractive at this time of year.

Quercus candicans Née

Mexico, Guatemala

A large spreading tree growing on mountain slopes, usually in humid areas, this species has stout downy shoots. It is widely distributed in Mexico, where it can reach 25 m tall with a trunk of more than 1 m diameter. The obovate leaves, edged with slender bristle-like teeth, are up to 25 cm long, glossy dark green above and densely covered with white hairs beneath. The young growth is attractively flushed with coppery red. The large, rounded acorns, about 2 cm across, ripen the second year and are borne singly or in clusters of up to three on a short, stout stalk.

There are splendid specimens at Hackfalls Arboretum in New Zealand, where it was introduced by Bob Berry of Gisborne, New Zealand, and where it has hybridised with some of the North American red oaks.

We have two established trees at Chevithorne Barton. They are probably the stars of the collection. Both were planted in 1992 from small plants supplied by James Harris of Mallet Court Nursery, Somerset. They have grown into handsome upright trees of 10.5 and 11 m, and show every sign of growing much taller. The taller one is the UK Champion Tree. One feature of this species is that the same plant can bear two differently shaped sorts of leaf (see illustrations, right). Although rather marginal in our climate, this tree has not suffered any frost damage for the last six years. They have probably benefited from global warming. The conclusion is that this tree is well worth trying in a protected position (sheltered from sub-zero winds) in the warmer counties.

We have since planted one or two further specimens in more exposed positions to see how they get on.

Mexico

This evergreen tree can reach 15 m or more in Mexico, where it is widely distributed, occurring mainly in oak/pine forests. The variable leaves are generally oblong to oblanceolate, to 15 cm or more in length, and with shallow lobes, bristle-tipped teeth or nearly entire. They are leathery in texture, glossy dark green above with deeply impressed veins and grey-white beneath. The acorns, up to 2 cm long, ripen the first year and are borne singly or in pairs on short stalks. In Mexico the leaves fall in late winter.

It has reached 8 m at Kew.

We only acquired this oak in 2007. It shows every sign of growing well in our climate. A previous tree, given to us as an acorn by James Reeve under the name *Q. sempervivens*, was later identified as *Q. castanea* by Allen Coombes in February 2008. It is a rather bushy tree (3 m in 2008), growing strongly in the area known as North of the Tapir Orchard, where it seems happy and hardy.

Hybrids of this species have been seen in Mexico and two similar ones have been collected by Allen Coombes. *Q. castanea × Q. eduardii* was collected in Zacatecas in 1996 and planted out at Chevithorne Barton five years later. It is quite vigorous but has been affected by frost damage fairly regularly. This cuts back the oak but does not kill it. After a warm but comparatively unsunny year, it is a healthy hardy tree about 1.5 m high.

Q. castanea × Q. sapotifolia was collected by Allen Coombes in Veracruz in 1995. Three specimens were planted here, two in open areas exposed to the wind and one in the more sheltered part of the garden wood. The latter grew rapidly to a decent 4 m, then it succumbed to a late spring frost and was cut back to the ground. The other two are affected by cold weather and need some hot summers to get established. The jury is out on whether this oak will become established, but it is worth trying because of its wonderful autumn colours.

top left: *Q. castanea × Q. eduardii*
bottom left: *Q. castanea*
right: *Q. castanea × Q. sapotifolia*

Quercus castaneifolia C.A. Mey.

Chestnut-leaved oak
E Caucasus, N Iran

A deciduous tree reaching heights of 40 m
or more in the forests bordering the Caspian
Sea. It is equally impressive in cultivation,
fast-growing and hardy. The oblong, taper-
pointed leaves to 20 cm long are glossy dark
green above, blue-grey and thinly hairy
beneath. Chestnut-like in appearance, they
are edged with numerous, pointed, triangular
teeth. The acorns ripen the second year. They
are up to 3.5 cm long and are borne in short-
stalked cups covered in bristly scales. This
species frequently produces acorns in this
country but they often give rise to hybrids
with *Q. cerris*. These hybrids resemble the
very variable *Q. cerris* but the leaves tend to
have more numerous and more regular lobes.

Introduced before 1846, it has reached
31 m at Kew.

These trees flourish at Chevithorne
Barton. We have three good specimens
planted between 1990 and 1994: all are
handsome at over 8.5 m tall and are well-
shaped, vigorous trees. However, one of the
most dramatic trees in our young collection
is a *Q. castaneifolia* 'Green Spire', a form with
upright branches selected by Hillier
Nurseries. Our tree has grown to 16 m in
twenty years and dominates the other oaks in
the area around the swimming pool. This oak
is hardy and elegant, and has a place in any
collection which has room for big trees.

Quercus cerris L.

Turkey oak
S & C Europe, Turkey

A familiar deciduous tree of the largest size, frequently reaching 30 m or more, this species is so commonly naturalised in Britain that it is often thought to be native, but is easily distinguished from our two native species (*Q. petraea* and *Q. robur*) by the downy shoots, the persistent stipules around the buds and the long scales on the acorn cup. The leaves are oblong to oval in outline, to 12 cm long and shallowly or deeply cut into pointed or rounded lobes. The acorns are up to 3 cm long and ripen the second year in a cup covered in slender scales.

The leaves are extremely variable in shape and some forms, with shallow rounded leaf lobes or short petioles, have been thought to be hybrids with *Q. robur*. Unfortunately this species is secondary host to the wasp that causes knopper gall, which disfigures so many acorns on *Q. robur*.

Introduced before 1735. A splendid tree, 36 m tall with a full crown, is at Knightshayes Court, 2 miles from Chevithorne Barton.

There were no Turkey oaks at Chevithorne Barton before we started collecting but several have now been planted, the tallest of which is about 8 m.

Several selections have been made, of which the most striking is 'Argenteovariegata', first described in 1877, in which the leaf margin is creamy yellow when the foliage is young, then turning to white. We have a good specimen here which was planted in 1989 and is now 7 m high. We also have various other cultivars, including the recent 'Wodan' which has deeper lobed leaves and goes a good yellow colour in autumn.

left: *Q. cerris* 'Argenteovariegata'
top right: *Q. cerris*
bottom right: *Q. cerris* 'Wodan'

Quercus chrysolepis Liebm.

Canyon live oak, Maul oak
SW United States, NW Mexico

This is the most common species, both in the wild and in cultivation, of section *Protobalanus*, which consists of only five species of evergreen trees or shrubs from California and northwestern Mexico. The oblong, pointed leaves up to 7 cm long are usually spiny toothed in young trees and entire on mature trees, but sometimes the latter have all spiny leaves. They are glossy green above with a dense covering of small golden hairs beneath when young which falls away to leave a smooth, bluish surface. The acorns are up to 3 cm long in a thick, corky cup and ripen the second year. They are rarely borne here unless several trees are grown together. Introduced by Charles Sargent of the Arnold Arboretum, Boston, USA, in 1877, it has reached 13 m at Kew.

We have one good specimen at Chevithorne Barton. It is a narrow compact tree of 8 m, happy and hardy in our climate.

Three other species in section *Protobalanus* are also cultivated.

Q. palmeri Engelm. (*Q. dunnii* Kellogg) (Palmer oak). SW United States (California, Arizona, New Mexico), Baja California. An evergreen shrub or small tree with rigidly spiny wavy-edged leaves covered with yellowish hairs beneath when young, later blue-green. The acorn cup is slightly flared so that it does tightly enclose the acorn. Plants in cultivation derive from a 1997 introduction. Acorns of this species have only been recently acquired here.

Q. tomentella Engelm. (Island live oak). California Channel islands, Guadalupe Island (Mexico). A large tree proving faster growing than *Q. chrysolepis* with rigid, glossy green leaves to 12 x 7 cm with deeply impressed veins ending in small teeth, grey and downy beneath. A threatened species in the wild, it has reached 7 m in at the Hillier Gardens following its introduction there in 1997. It is listed as Vulnerable in the Red List of Oaks. Seed collected from cultivated plants in California can give the hybrid *Q. chrysolepis* × *Q. tomentella*, which also occurs in the wild with the parents. This hybrid does well here and one planted in 2002 is 1.5 m high.

Q. vacciniifolia Kellogg (Huckleberry oak). W United States (California, Oregon, Nevada). This is a small shrub with leaves to 3.5 cm long that lack the golden hairs found on the underside in *Q. chrysolepis*. It grows on rocky slopes and in forests in the mountains. It is associated with *Ceanothus prostratus* in the High Sierra of California (see *The Plantsman*, June 2008). Introduced in 1900. One planted in the rockery here is well established. It is not expected to get very large.

top left: *Q. chrysolepis*
bottom left: *Q. palmeri*
centre: *Q. chrysolepis* × *Q. tomentella*
top right: *Q. vacciniifolia*
bottom right: *Q. tomentella*

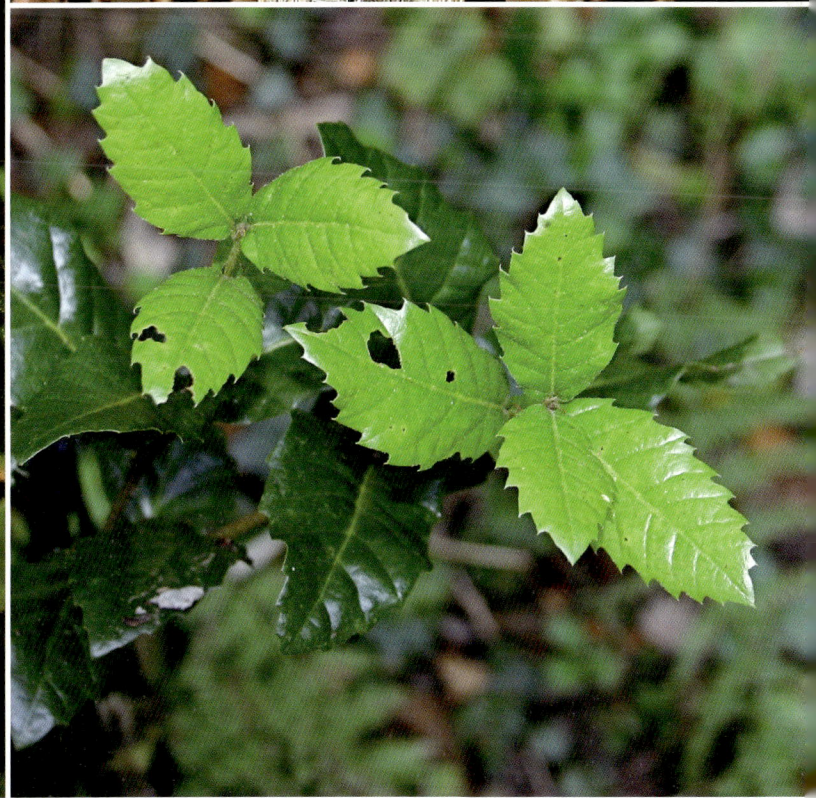

Kermes oak
Mediterranean region

This large evergreen shrub or small tree can reach 3 m or more and is a familiar sight in many parts of the Mediterranean region, where it grows on rocky soils. The oval to oblong rigid leaves, glossy green on both sides, are up to 4 cm long and are edged with sharp, spiny teeth. The acorns, which ripen the second year, are up to 3 cm or more long and are borne in a cup that is rough with spine-tipped scales.

This species is variable in habit, and forms which make good-sized trees occur particularly in the east of the range, in Greece, Turkey and the Near East. In the mountains, it is often reduced to a dwarf shrub growing over the rocks. Insects that breed on this oak in its native habitat are the source of Kermes red dye.

Cultivated since the 17th century, it has reached 9 m at Borde Hill, Haywards Heath, West Sussex.

There is one small tree at Chevithorne Barton, 1.5 m in height, which appears to be hardy in our climate.

Q. coccifera subsp. **calliprinos** (Webb) Holmboe (*Q. calliprinos* Webb). Known as the Palestine oak, this makes a large tree in the eastern Mediterranean region and has larger leaves and acorn cups. There are three specimens here which seem quite hardy. The tallest, planted out in 2006, is 1.5 m and growing well. It is evergreen in our climate.

Q. coccifera subsp. **rivasmartinezii** J.H. Capelo & J.C. Costa (*Q. z* (J.H. Capelo & J.C. Costa) J.H. Capelo & J.C. Costa). This form, found in a small area near the coast in southern Portugal, makes a tree to 15 m or more. It was introduced in 2001 (the same year in which it was named), when a group

from the International Oak Society visited southern Spain and Portugal. Young plants from this collection have attractive coppery young foliage. Two vigorous young plants were put into the rockery three years ago. They have grown fast into dense bushes about 1.5 m in height. One has now been moved to the woodland garden, a more suitable long term position. This is a healthy, attractive oak.

Q. aucheri Jaub. & Spach. This uncommon species is a small tree or shrub growing only in coastal areas of southwest Turkey and some of the Aegean islands. It differs from *Q. coccifera* in having the undersides of the leaves, the cup scales and acorns densely grey hairy. It has been in cultivation since at least 1999 but is slower growing than *Q. coccifera*, and appears to be less hardy. It is listed as Near Threatened in the Red List of Oaks. There is one small shrub in the rockery which looks established.

left: *Q. coccifera*
top centre, top right: *Q. coccifera* subsp. *calliprinos*
bottom centre: *Q. coccifera* subsp. *rivasmartinezii*
bottom right: *Q. aucheri*

Quercus coccinea Münchh.

Section Lobatae

Scarlet oak
E United States

A large deciduous tree found mainly on well-drained soils in deciduous woods on upland sites, this is among the best species for autumn colour here. The leaves are deeply cut into seven–nine lobes which broaden towards the end and divide into several bristle-tipped teeth. They are glossy dark green above, paler and glossy beneath, with inconspicuous tufts of hair in the vein axils and turn scarlet in autumn. The nearly rounded acorns about 2 cm long ripen the second year and are borne singly or in pairs in short-stalked hemispherical cups.

Introduced in 1691.

This oak is perfectly at home at Chevithorne Barton and we have a good young tree on the slope above the Millennium Bridge.

'Splendens' is a form selected before 1914 for its particularly good autumn colour. We have two established trees of this cultivar: the oldest, planted in 1988 in the Tapir Orchard, is a well-developed 10 m-high specimen. It has reached 28 m at Windsor Great Park, Berkshire.

all: *Q. coccinea* 'Splendens'

Quercus conspersa Benth.

S Mexico, C America

A tree reaching 10–15 m tall in the wild,
where the leaves turn yellow in winter before
falling. The leathery leaves are ovate to
elliptic, up to 15 cm long and 8 cm wide.
Variable in shape, they are often entire,
ending in a bristle-tipped point or they can
have up to five or more bristle-tipped teeth
on each side. They are dark green above, paler
beneath, and nearly smooth but with tufts of
hairs in the axils of the main veins. Acorns
ripen the second year and are borne singly or
in pairs on a short stalk, about 1 cm long in a
hemispherical cup 2 cm across. This species is
confused with, and sometimes difficult to
distinguish from, *Q. acutifolia*.

We have two good specimens of this oak
at Chevithorne Barton. The tallest, planted in
1992, is 7 m high, and although it loses its
leaves comparatively early, it is quite hardy
in our climate.

Quercus crassifolia Humb. & Bonpl.

Section *Lobatae*

Mexico, C America

A distinct, usually easily recognised, tree reaching 20 m or more in Mexico where it is widely distributed, particularly in colder localities. The rigid, leathery leaves are elliptic to obovate, often narrowed to the base and with bristle-tipped teeth above the widest part of the leaf. They emerge densely covered in velvety red hairs, becoming glossy blackish green above and covered with a thick layer of pale brown hairs beneath. In the wild, the leaves usually fall late in late winter: here they remain until early spring. Acorns ovoid to 2 cm long, ripening the second year, borne singly or in clusters of up to four on short stalks.

Introduced by George Hinton in 1939 (Hinton 6402) – a tree from the original introduction is still alive at Caerhays, Cornwall. It has reached 13 m at Kew.

At Chevithorne Barton, this very distinct oak is quite hardy. We have three good trees, two in the open, one is in a sheltered position. The latter has a handsome habit, striking, slightly spongy bark and thick leaves. It has grown to over 10 m in about eight years and looks set to continue growing. The other trees are more conventionally shaped. All three seem to be established.

C Mexico

An evergreen tree reaching 20 m in the wild where it is often found in relatively cold and dry areas. The leathery, narrow-elliptic to oblong leaves up to 10 cm long and 3 cm wide are untoothed, except for a small point at the tip, and have a recurved margin. They are glossy dark green above with numerous, deeply impressed spreading veins, and densely covered with yellow-brown hairs beneath, at least when young. Acorns ovoid to 2 cm long ripening the second year, the cup 2 cm wide with a characteristic inrolled margin. This species can be confused with *Q. mexicana* but the cup will help distinguish it. The leaves turn yellow and fall in late winter in Mexico.

Introduced by Carl Hartweg in 1839, it has reached 19 m at Carclew, Truro, Cornwall.

We have two established trees at Chevithorne Barton. The seed was acquired from Silvia Romero of Mexico in 1995 and the trees were eventually planted out in the Walnut Orchard and Rifle Range. They are now about 5 m high, well shaped but somewhat slow growing and lose their leaves in late autumn.

Q. ×dysophylla Benth. (*Q. crassifolia* × *Q. crassipes*). This hybrid can often be found in areas of Mexico where the parent species grow together, and sometimes when only one of them is present. The leaves are very variable in shape but are often similar to those of *Q. crassipes*, though broader and more densely hairy beneath. They are also often toothed.

It was first introduced by Allen Coombes in 1995 and grows vigorously in cultivation. We had a plant from this introduction which grew rapidly to about 6 m and was one of our star exhibits. It snapped off at the roots one stormy night in 2006. Subsequent investigation established that it had a very inadequate root system for such a vigorous fast growing tree so it would never have reached maturity. We have recently acquired a good replacement about 1 m high which has survived its first winter satisfactorily: we hope it will emulate its predecessor.

top left, top centre: *Q.* ×*dysophylla*
bottom left, bottom centre, top and bottom right: *Q. crassipes*

Quercus crispipilis Trel.

Section *Lobatae*

S Mexico, Guatemala

A vigorous evergreen tree reaching 20 m or more and found at high altitudes in tropical regions. The glossy green, leathery leaves are elliptic to oblong or obovate and untoothed or with a single small point at the tip. They have distinctly impressed veins on the upper surface and are tomentose on the underside. Acorns ovoid to 2 cm long, ripening the second year, borne singly or in small clusters on short stalks.

Introduced to New Zealand from Chiapas, southern Mexico by Bob Berry in 1982, several fine trees from this and later collections grow at Hackfalls Arboretum. It was introduced to Britain by Guy Sternberg who collected it in Guatemala in 1998.

At Chevithorne Barton, we have a good specimen, which came from Bob Berry in New Zealand via the late Jo Earle of Ryme Intrinseca, Dorset. It is a vigorous small-leafed tree in a very sheltered position, about 4 m high. It is not completely hardy and sometimes gets affected by frost.

Daimio oak
NE Asia

A large tree reaching 20 m or more in the wild where it grows, from Japan to Korea and China. The stout, densely hairy shoots bear large obovate, short-stalked leaves to 30 cm long or more, edged with shallow, rounded lobes. Dark green above and often rough to the touch, they are densely hairy beneath. Acorns to 2 cm long, ripening the first year, the cup densely covered in slender, recurved scales.

Introduced in 1830, it has reached 18 m in Ireland. Plants grown from garden seed are sometimes hybrids with *Q. robur*.

At Chevithorne Barton we have three specimens, one planted in 1998 which has developed into a classically shaped tree over 11 m high. There is some minor die-back each year but none that cannot be dealt with. The second specimen was planted in 1986 and has developed into a small shrub only 2 m high. The third specimen is much younger and is growing well. This is a distinctive species, which deserves wider recognition.

We also have a plant suspected to be *Q. dentata* × *Q. malacotricha*, a delicate natural hybrid, which is susceptible to frost but when it is not held back turns a most glorious red in autumn.

'Carl Ferris Miller' is a selection of *Q. dentata* that grows particularly well. It was propagated from a plant collected in Korea in 1976 by Robert and Jelena de Belder of Hemelrijk, Belgium. 'Pinnatifida', described from Japan in 1875 is a slow-growing form with deeply cut leaves. We have small trees at Chevithorne Barton of each of these selections. I met the late Carl Ferris Miller in the 1990s in his office in Seoul. Unfortunately we did not have time to visit his famous arboretum, Chollipo, which he built on the coast, five hours south of Seoul.

Q. fabri Hance, from China, grows to 20 m or more in the wild where it is widely distributed in forests in the mountains. The young shoots are densely hairy, eventually becoming smooth. Leaves obovate, up to 15 cm long and 8 cm across, on a short petiole to 5 mm long, edged with about ten shallow, rounded teeth on each side. They are glossy dark green above, grey and hairy beneath and can turn red in autumn. Acorns to 2.5 cm long, ripening the first year, up to four borne in hemispherical cups on a short stalk to 4 cm long.

Introduced in 1995 by John Gammon of Birchfleet Nursery, Hampshire, and Susan Cooper of Worcestershire, and also by later collectors. It has reached about 3 m at the Hillier Gardens but seems to thrive more in regions with hot summers. The specific epithet is sometimes misspelled 'fabrei' or 'faberi'. At Chevithorne Barton we have three small specimens of this oak all planted in the last few years. They are about 1.5 and 2 m high and so far seem quite happy.

top, bottom: *Q. dentata*

Quercus dentata Thunb.

Continued from previous page

Q. yunnanensis Franch. (*Q. dentata* susbp. *yunnanensis* (Franch.) Menitsky) is similar to *Q. dentata* but has pointed leaf lobes and smaller, upright scales on the acorn cups. It is native to southwest China (Sichuan and Yunnan). There are two young trees of this oak in the collection which, although slightly delicate, are both 2 m high and reasonably well established.

left: *Q. dentata* 'Carl Ferris Miller'
right: *Q. dentata* × *Q. yunnanensis*

Quercus deserticola Trel.

C & W Mexico

A small tree up to 10 m tall, often less, with a shrubby and usually wide-spreading habit. It is found in pine/oak woods in dry, rocky places. The densely hairy shoots bear obovate to oblong leaves up to 10 cm long and 5 cm wide. They are bronze when young and densely hairy. Mature leaves are dark grey-green above and hairy on both sides, with up to six shallow pointed lobes on each margin, or sometimes entire. Acorns ovoid to 2 cm long, ripening the first year, half included in a scaly cup to 1.5 cm across, borne singly or in small clusters on a stalk to 2.5 cm long.

Introduced by Allen Coombes in 1995.

At Chevithorne Barton, we have one tree planted about ten years ago in the Rifle Range. It was slow to get established, but since then has put on significant growth. New growth is often a spectacular display of pink shoots. This is probably the only specimen in the UK.

China

An evergreen tree that can reach 10 m or more, though it can sometimes be much smaller and shrubby in exposed rocky places. Shoots downy at first, becoming smooth. The leathery, obovate leaves are up to 7 cm long and are edged with small teeth towards the tip. They are grey-hairy when young, becoming glossy dark green and smooth above. Acorns to 2 cm long, ripening the second year, borne singly or in pairs in cups densely covered in slender scales.

Introduced to Kew in 1992, it was later received by Hillier Gardens in 1998 as *Q. spinosa*, where it has reached 3.5 m.

At Chevithorne Barton, we have one attractive tree planted in 1991. It is a vigorous and hardy tree about 4 m high and in most years is the first tree in the collection to produce new leaves. We also have some smaller, newer specimens. This oak is well worth growing.

top left: acorns photographed in Yunnan, China

NW Mexico

A native of oak/pine woods and canyons, this spreading tree has stout shoots densely covered in grey hairs. Leaves lance-shaped to narrow ovate, to 8 cm long and 3 cm wide, tapered to a fine, bristle-tipped point, entire or with a few marginal teeth, rounded to shallowly heart-shaped at the base. Mature leaves are glossy dark green above, and grey or white-tomentose beneath. With age, the tomentum on the underside of the leaf starts to fall away and rubs off easily, leaving the surface glossy green. Acorns ovoid, ripening the first year, and borne singly or in pairs on a short stalk.

Introduced by Sir Harold Hillier to the Hillier Gardens in 1979, where it has reached 7 m.

We have one good specimen planted in 1991, which is 8 m high. It seems completely hardy and is evergreen.

Northern pin oak
Great Lakes region of N America

A fast-growing deciduous tree reaching 20 m in the wild, where it can often be found in woods on well-drained soils. The leaves are elliptic in outline, up to 15 cm long and deeply cut into five–seven lobes that divide at the tips into bristle-tipped teeth. Glossy green and glabrous on both sides except for very small tufts of hairs in the leaf axils beneath, they turn red in autumn. Acorns ovoid to 2 cm long, ripening the second year. It is closely related to *Q. coccinea* and *Q. palustris*.

Introduced in 1902, it has reached 18 m at the Hillier Gardens.

We have one of these trees at Chevithorne Barton planted in 1991. It has grown fairly fast and is about 7 m high, and seems quite happy in our climate. The cultivar 'Hemelrijk' was selected at Hemelrijk, Belgium, for its very good and reliable red autumn colour. The original plant came from Hillier Nurseries. We have two fine examples of this tree, of which the tallest is about 9 m high.

Quercus emoryi Torr.

Emory oak
SW United States, North Mexico

A slow-growing evergreen or semi-evergreen tree reaching 15 m or more in the wild, where it grows on dry slopes, grasslands and oak/pine woodland. The rigid shoots, often reddish when young, bear glossy green oblong leaves to 9 cm long. Downy when young, they become smooth above and sparsely hairy beneath, and are edged with sparse teeth or entire. Acorns ovoid to oblong, to 2 cm long, ripening the first year, and borne singly or in pairs in shallow cups. It has reached 8 m at Hillier Gardens.

We have two small young specimens of this elegant oak at Chevithorne Barton.

Q. hypoleucoides A. Camus. The Silverleaf oak from Southwestern United States and northern Mexico is an evergreen tree to 10 m tall with leathery, dark green, entire or spine-toothed narrow elliptic leaves to 10 cm long, densely and permanently white tomentose beneath. The acorns can ripen in the first or second year. It is not common in cultivation but a tree planted in 1973 has reached 10 m at the Hillier Gardens. Some plants seen are the hybrid described below, but we do have a small specimen of true *Q. hypoleucoides*.

Q. emoryi × Q. hypoleucoides seems to be the identity of a plant that has been distributed as *Q. hypoleucoides*. It is more vigorous than either parent in cultivation and has leathery, untoothed leaves, reddish when young and densely covered in grey hairs beneath that rub off easily. A tree planted in 1968 has reached 11 m at the Hillier Gardens. We have a tree of this hybrid here, which is well established and attractive at about 5 m.

top left, bottom left: *Q. emoryi*
top right, bottom centre: *Q. emoryi × Q. hypoleucoides*
bottom right: true *Q. hypoleucoides*

Quercus eugeniifolia Liebm.

Section *Lobatae*

C America, S Mexico

The tree in cultivation under this name in several collections was grown from seeds collected by Allen Coombes in Veracruz, southern Mexico, but what is probably the same species was introduced earlier to Kew. It has proved fast growing and hardy and has reached 8 m at the Hillier Gardens. The slender, ridged shoots bear lance-shaped, usually untoothed leaves to 18 × 4 cm, ending in a fine point, dark green above, paler beneath, glossy on both sides. Several flushes of coppery red young foliage are produced each year and at the Hillier Gardens the last flush can be damaged by winter frosts.

Q. eugeniifolia as originally described from Costa Rica, is a species from Central America that has distinctly toothed leaves and the plants in gardens represent a new, as yet undescribed species.

We have a good specimen of this unnamed species at Chevithorne Barton. It is in a protected position about 7 m high, with very attractive young leaves and is almost hardy. Another introduction of this species was made by Allen Coombes from Hidalgo, Mexico, in 2008.

Portuguese oak
Spain, Portugal, N Africa

A deciduous or semi-evergreen tree growing to 20 m tall, sometimes shrubby, the young shoots densely hairy later becoming glabrous. The leaves are variable in shape and size, from ovate to oblong or obovate, and up to 10 cm long but often less. They are glossy dark green or grey-green above and blue-green beneath, hairy at least when young. Acorns usually oblong to 3 cm long, ripening the first year, carried singly or in pairs on a short stalk to 2.5 cm long.

Introduced in 1835, it has reached 16 m at the National Botanic Gardens, Glasnevin, Dublin.

At Chevithorne Barton, we have two well-established trees of 9 and 11 m. A plant distributed recently as *Q. ×hispanica* 'Brünn', propagated from a tree at Brno Botanic Garden, Czech Republic, appears to be *Q. faginea*. We also have one of these and it is growing well.

This is a variable species in its range. *Q. faginea* subsp. *alpestris* (Boiss.) Maire grows at high altitudes in southern Spain and has relatively small leaves. It is listed as Endangered in the Red List of Oaks. We have one small specimen 2.2 m high.

Q. faginea subsp. *broteroi* (Cout.) A. Camus has broad leaves, densely white tomentose beneath, and occurs in the southern part of the range. We have one small but vigorous young tree of 1.2 m in height.

Quercus falcata Michx.

Southern red oak, Spanish oak
E United States

A large deciduous tree reaching 30 m or more in height and often found on dry soils on hills and ridges in oak/pine forests. Young shoots densely covered in rusty coloured hairs. The large glossy dark green leaves, felted beneath, are up to 25 cm or more long, have a characteristic rounded base, up to three deep lobes on each side and a long terminal lobe. Each lobe ends in one to several bristle-tipped teeth. Leaves of the second flush have more lobes. The nearly rounded acorns are about 1.5 cm long and ripen the second year, singly or in pairs on a short stalk.

Introduced in 1763, it has reached 21 m at Kew.

We have two examples of this oak at Chevithorne Barton. The best is a classically shaped tree in the Kitchen Garden 8 m in height.

Q. pagoda Raf. (*Q. falcata* var. *pagodifolia* Elliott). The Cherrybark oak, also from the Eastern United States, grows in more fertile, moister soils. It differs in its cherry-like bark and the more regularly lobed leaves with a tapered or cut-off base. It grows vigorously in cultivation and has reached 22 m at Syon Park, Middlesex. We have three trees of this species.

top left, right: *Q. falcata*
bottom left: *Q. pagoda*

SW China, N Thailand

This evergreen tree can reach 15 m or more in the wild but is often seen as a small tree or large shrub growing in evergreen oak and pine forests. The young shoots are densely covered in grey hairs becoming glabrous. Leaves elliptic to obovate, to 10 cm long, edged with short teeth above the centre. They are rigid and leathery, glossy dark green above and densely covered beneath with a thick, bright white tomentum. Acorns ovoid-oblong to 1.5 cm long but often much less, ripening the first or second year, and are borne singly or in small clusters on a short stalk.

Introduced in 1990 or before, it has reached 6 m at Tregrehan, Cornwall.

We have two small trees of about 2 m at Chevithorne Barton and they look to be established.

Georgia oak
SE United States

A deciduous spreading tree, sometimes
shrubby, reaching 10 m or more. This is a rare
species growing on granite outcrops in
Georgia and Alabama. The glabrous, reddish
brown shoots bear leaves to 10 cm long,
tapered at the base and deeply cut into three–
five lobes that end in bristle-tipped teeth.
They are glossy green and glabrous on both
sides except for tufts of hairs in the axils of the
veins beneath. Acorns ovoid to nearly
spherical, to 1.5 cm long, ripening the second
year. It is listed as Endangered in the Red List
of Oaks.

E Mexico

A large evergreen tree reaching 25 m or more in the wild, where it grows in humid forests. Shoots are glabrous and ridged. The short-stalked elliptic to obovate, glabrous, leathery leaves are up to 20 cm long with few teeth towards the end. They are bronze when young, becoming glossy dark green above and blue-green beneath. Acorns large to 4 cm long, nearly rounded, borne singly or in clusters of up to three on a short, stout stalk, ripening the first year and mostly enclosed in the cup.

Although having a wide distribution in Mexico, this is listed as Vulnerable in the Red List of Oaks. It has mainly been collected in Veracruz, from where it was introduced by Jim Russell of Castle Howard, North Yorkshire, in 1984. Collections from further north may prove hardier, but being a white oak it does best in areas with hot summers.

We have three small trees of this oak at Chevithorne Barton, the biggest about 3.5 m high. It is slightly delicate but is worth trying in a sheltered position anywhere in the south of England.

Quercus gilva Blume

Japan, Taiwan, S China

A large evergreen tree reaching 30 m in the wild, where it is found in evergreen forests in the mountains. Young shoots densely covered in yellow-brown hairs. The elliptic to oblanceolate leaves up to 12 cm long are taper-pointed and edged with sharp teeth above the middle. They are dark green above with a dense covering of yellow-brown hairs beneath. Acorns are up to 2 cm long borne in a cup with six–eight concentric rings and ripen the first year. In recent years, some plants distributed under this name have proved to be *Q. glauca*. Surprisingly rare in cultivation in this country, it has reached 4 m at Kew.

We have three examples of this oak at Chevithorne Barton, the biggest about 2 m tall. It is not as delicate as it looks.

C Mexico

A large evergreen tree to 30 m or more in the wild, where it occurs in the mountains at altitudes of 2,000 m and above. The dark green, oblanceolate, leathery leaves are up to 10 cm long and edged with shallow, rounded lobes above the middle, below which they taper to a rounded base. Some forms have unlobed leaves. The edge of the leaf is characteristically turned over, giving it a distinct narrow dark green margin when viewed from beneath. Acorns ovoid, about 1.5 cm long, ripening the first year and borne singly or in clusters of up to three on a short stalk.

Introduced in about 1839, it has reached 8 m at Kew. This hardy species can produce acorns in this country. When sown, however, they usually turn out to be hybrids with *Q. robur*. A tree suspected to be of this parentage has reached 10 m at Hillier Gardens.

We have one good example of this oak at Chevithorne Barton. It seems hardy and grows well but slowly, and is about 4 m high. It produced acorns in 2005 which, unsurprisingly, gave rise to hybrids with *Q. robur*.

Quercus greggii (A. DC.) Trel.

Mexico

A small evergreen tree to 10 m or more, smaller and shrubby at high altitudes and in the north of its range. It is usually found in oak/pine forests in mountain areas. Young shoots densely hairy. Leaves ovate to obovate, thickly leathery, to 7 cm long and 5 cm across. They are glossy dark green above with deeply impressed veins, shallowly lobed above the middle, the lobes ending in short, bristle-tipped points and covered beneath with dense whitish or pale brown hairs. Acorns ovoid to 2 cm long, ripening the first year.

Introduced from Mexico by Sir Harold Hillier in 1979. A plant from this collection still grows at Kew.

There is a small tree of this species at Chevithorne Barton, planted in 2008.

Himalaya, SE Asia

A large deciduous tree growing to 25 m tall and found in mixed forests over a wide area. Grey-hairy shoots. The obovate, short-stalked leaves to 20 cm or more long are pointed at the tip and narrowed to the base, and are edged with shallow lobes. They are dark green and nearly smooth above when mature, grey-green and densely hairy beneath at least when young. Acorns about 2 cm long, borne singly or in clusters of up to three, and ripening the first year.

Introduced to Kew in 1992. A collection by John Gammon, in 1997, has reached 2.5 m at Hillier Gardens.

A tree has been at Chevithorne Barton for five years. Affected by frost in the first three years, it is now growing vigorously and is about 2.5 m tall. We also have a seedling from James MacEwen, collected in Bhutan.

Quercus hemisphaerica Bartram ex Willd.

Section *Lobatae*

Darlington oak,
SE United States

An evergreen or semi-evergreen tree reaching 35 m tall and found on well-drained sandy soils. Shoots glabrous, bearing narrow elliptic to oblanceolate leathery leaves to 12 cm long, usually pointed at the tip and entire or with a single shallow lobe on one side. Leaves on the second flush are often more prominently toothed. They are bronze when young, becoming glossy dark green above and more or less glabrous on both sides. Acorns nearly rounded to hemispherical, to 1.5 cm long, ripening the second year and borne singly or in pairs on a very short stalk.

This species has been commonly confused with *Q. laurifolia*, which differs in the leaves being usually rounded at the tip, and occurs in different habitats.

Introduced in about 1980 by Sir Harold Hillier to Hillier Gardens where it has reached 12 m.

There are three trees at Chevithorne Barton, the biggest of which is 5.5 m. They are multi-stemmed, a bit bush-like, grow relatively slowly but are hardy and rather distinctive. The leaves tend to go quite a good yellowish/brown and stay on the tree until around Christmas. This is a useful and hardy tree.

Quercus ×hispanica Lam.

(*Q. cerris* × *Q. suber*)
S Europe

A vigorous and large semi-evergreen tree reaching up to 30 m tall, the bark corky in some forms. Leaves to 12 cm long, very variable, usually ovate with a pointed tip and edged with triangular, pointed lobes. They are dark green above and grey with hairs beneath. Acorns to 2.5 cm long, ripening the second year and borne in a cup densely covered in narrow bristly scales. We have various cultivars of this hybrid.

Q. ×hispanica occurs in the wild where the parent species grow (or used to grow) together. 'Ambrozyana', raised at Arboretum Mlyňany in Slovakia prior to 1909, has very distinct fissured bark.

'Fulhamensis' is a selection named in 1838 from a tree that grew in the Whitley and Osborn Nursery in Fulham, west London. 'Lucombeana' (Lucombe oak) is the original form raised by William Lucombe of Exeter in about 1763 from seed of *Q. cerris*, but many plants under this name are probably seedlings. One tree, planted here about 1989, is 9 m tall. There are wonderful specimens of this tree along the South Devon and Cornwall coast, e.g., at Powderham and Chudleigh.

'Wageningen', described from the Netherlands in 1980, appears more close to *Q. trojana*. One tree, planted about 1989, is 9 m tall. 'Waasland Select', propagated from a plant at Hof ter Saksen, The Netherlands, and only formally described in 2004, has leaves with pointed lobes, often with a long, entire terminal lobe with a pointed tip. It is usually placed here but may be a form of *Q. ilex*.

top left, centre: *Q. ×hispanica* 'Lucombeana'
bottom left: *Q. ×hispanica* 'Fulhamensis'
right: *Q. ×hispanica* 'Ambrozyana'

Quercus ilex L.

Holm oak, Evergreen oak
Mediterranean region, Turkey

This familiar large tree is the most commonly grown evergreen oak in Britain. The leaves are very variable in shape and size. Frequently ovate and up to 8 cm long, they are entire or edged with sharp teeth. Densely covered with white hairs on both side as they emerge, they become dark green and smooth above and densely grey-hairy beneath. Leaves on sucker shoots from the base can be quite different, large, spine-toothed and green beneath. Acorns ovoid to 2 cm long, ripening the first year in cups covered in appressed hairy scales.

Cultivated since the 16th century, this species has become naturalised in southern Britain and has reached 27 m at Bicton Park in Devon.

There were no old trees at Chevithorne Barton but six were planted in 1991, the largest is now about 8 m tall.

'Fordii' is an old selection described in 1843 with narrow, wavy-edged leaves. Planted here in 1989 it has made an upward-growing, compact bush about 3 m tall.

Q. rotundifolia Lam. (Q. ilex var. *ballota* (Desf.) A. DC., *Q. ilex* var. *rotundifolia* (Lam.) Trab.). This native of southwest Spain and south Portugal is a close relative of *Q. ilex* but has large, sweet acorns that are eaten by pigs that give the famous Jamón Ibérico de Bellota. The acorns are also used to make a liqueur in Spain. It is not common in cultivation and has reached 16 m at Westonbirt Arboretum, Gloucestershire. It has been confused with *Q. ilex* 'Rotundifolia' and is listed as Near Threatened in the Red List of Oaks. The largest here is about 4 m tall.

left: *Q. rotundifolia*
centre: *Q. ilex*
right: *Q. ilex* 'Fordii'

Quercus ilicifolia Wangenh.

Section *Lobatae*

Bear oak, Scrub oak
NE United States

A small deciduous tree to 8 m tall, often less, usually branching low down, or a shrub sometimes forming dense thickets. Young shoots densely covered in grey hairs. The slender-stalked elliptic to obovate leaves are up to 10 cm long and deeply to rather shallowly cut into three–seven lobes, each ending in bristle-tipped teeth. They emerge red-flushed and hairy on both sides, becoming smooth and dark green above, with a dense grey tomentum beneath. Acorns ovoid to nearly spherical to 1.5 cm long, ripening the second year and borne singly or in small clusters on short stalks. It has grown to about 4 m here at Chevithorne Barton.

'Tromp Ball' ('Nana') is a compact shrubby form propagated from a plant of about 2 by 5 m at Arboretum Trompenburg, Rotterdam, The Netherlands. It is more vigorous and open in habit when grafted, and has reached 2.5 m here.

left: *Q. ilicifolia* 'Tromp Ball'
right: *Q. ilicifolia*

Quercus imbricaria Michx.

Shingle oak
E United States

A fast-growing deciduous tree of medium size reaching about 25 m tall and found in a variety of habitats from hill slopes and ridges to moist valley bottoms. The elliptic leaves to 20 cm long are untoothed and have a single bristle-point at the rounded tip. They are glossy dark green above and green beneath with a dense covering of fine hairs and turn red-brown in autumn. Acorns ovoid to nearly rounded, to 1.8 cm long, ripening the second year and borne singly or in pairs on a short stalk. The common name and specific epithet derive from the use of the wood by early pioneers to make roof shingles.

Introduced in 1786 by John Fraser of the American Nursery, Sloane Square, London, it has reached 27 m at Syon Park, Middlesex.

There are six trees here at Chevithorne Barton, the largest being 8 m tall. They grow vigorously and sometimes give good autumn colour. Two semi-mature trees were planted on the top side of the oak bridge. They are all right but have not grown much.

Q. ×leana Nutt. (*Q. imbricaria* × *Q. velutina*). A naturally occurring hybrid found with the parents, this can resemble *Q. imbricaria* but has broader usually lobed leaves. Other forms can resemble *Q. velutina* but with less deeply lobed leaves. Long cultivated, it has reached 24 m at Tregrehan, Cornwall. A wide-spreading tree here is about 3.5 m tall.

left: *Q. imbricaria*
right: *Q. ×leana*

Quercus incana Bartram

Bluejack oak
SE United States

A small deciduous tree, sometimes shrubby, to about 10 m tall and usually found on sandy soils. The rigid shoots are densely covered in grey hairs when young and the bark soon cracks into small dark squares. Leaves elliptic to obovate, to 10 cm long, narrowed to the base, untoothed or occasionally with few shallow lobes and ending in a short point. They are blue-green to glossy green above and densely covered in white hairs beneath. Acorns ovoid to nearly rounded, about 1.5 cm long, ripening the second year in a short-stalked or sessile cup.

Although hardy, this species is rare in cultivation and slow-growing but has reached more than 4 m eight years after planting at the Hillier Gardens where it was first grown in the 1970s. It prefers a well drained soil in a warm, sunny site.

There are two trees at Chevithorne Barton, one is doing well, the other is rather untidy and has been forced to grow upwards but is now also doing well at 4.5 m in a sheltered spot near the Tapir Orchard.

SE Europe, Turkey

A large, semi-evergreen shrub or small tree to 10 m or more, closely related to *Q. faginea* from which it differs chiefly in its glabrous or nearly glabrous spine-toothed leaves and branches. Leaves to 5 cm long on petioles to 5 mm. The galls produced by this oak are used in dyeing and also in medicine.

Introduced in 1822 and first cultivated in 1850. It has reached 20 m at Syon Park, Middlesex. This species is rare in cultivation.

We have one specimen at Chevithorne Barton, which came from seed collected by a team from Kew in mixed deciduous woodland at 100 m in Isparta Province, Yusekharman, Turkey in September 1990. Normally found on rocky mountain slopes up to 1,000 m, we have planted our specimen in a normal garden situation and it seems tolerant of our climate. It is now about 3 m, healthy and happy, but in our conditions seems to be a slow grower.

Q. infectoria subsp. ***veneris*** (A. Kern.) Meikle (*Q. boissieri* Reuter, *Q. infectoria* subsp. *boissieri* (Reuter) O. Schwarz. This eastern variant from Southwest Asia (Cyprus, southeast Turkey, Israel to Iran and Iraq) differs in its usually greater size and larger, longer-stalked leaves. There are two specimens here, one planted in 2001 in the area known as North of the Tapir Orchard, now about 1 m, so a slow grower, but healthy and hardy in a rather shady position, the other in the Rookery, planted 1997.

Mexico, C America

A large deciduous tree to 30 m with branchlets covered in dense, yellow tomentum becoming glabrous, glaucous or grey in second year. The large and attractive leaves are elliptic to obovate, thick and hard, the upper surface shiny and glabrous, the lower surface dull and tomentose. The young foliage is densely covered with deep red velvety hairs when it emerges. This species is noted for its enormous acorns, which are ovoid to globose and are, with a cup up to 12 cm in diameter, the largest of any oak species. Unusually for an oak, they germinate from the base of the acorn. It is listed as Near Threatened in the Red List of Oaks.

According to Allen and Maricela Coombes, this is one of most spectacular big trees in Mexico, where it is a rare species found in cloud forest between 900 and 1,400 m. This would indicate that it is not hardy in the UK, and we have found this out the hard way at Chevithorne Barton.

We first acquired acorns in 1995 after Allen Coombes's trip to Veracruz, Mexico. Allen collected the acorns from trees that he found growing in moist, subtropical woodland around the bottom of a river valley at a little over 1,100 m. From this collection, a handful of acorns germinated and from these we planted one tree in a woodland setting. It survived one winter but succumbed to a late frost in April 2006. The other plant is kept in the greenhouse and is doing well.

Allen recounts that he spotted the tree and its huge acorns but could not reach them as they were 15 m above the ground. Although some were downed by throwing sticks, most acorns were collected by two local boys, who later brought handfuls of them to a nearby café, where the group was having lunch, in return for a few coins.

There is an impressive specimen from the same collection in the Temperate House at the Royal Botanic Gardens, Kew, where it was touching the roof after being planted in 1998 but has since been trimmed.

This is a most attractive species but marginally hardy in Devon. It grows well at Tregrehan in coastal Cornwall and in southwest France. I will try again with another tree in the hope that it will do better with global warming. This oak will always be noted for the size of its acorns, the biggest of which are the size of a small saucer: quite different from any other acorn I have seen.

left: New growth on *Q. insignis*
top right: *Q. insignis* growing in the Green House at Chevithorne Barton
bottom right: *Q. insignis*, Jalisco, Mexico

Quercus intricata Trel.

Coahuila scrub oak
Texas, North Mexico

An intricately branched evergreen shrub to about 2 m tall with densely hairy shoots forming thickets on mountain slopes. The thick leathery leaves, oblong to ovate, to 2.5 cm long, are glossy dark green with scattered hairs above and have a dense felt of white hairs beneath. They are borne on a very short stalk and have a wavy or sparsely toothed margin, which is often rolled under the leaf. Acorns ovoid, about 1 cm long, borne singly or in pairs on a short stalk, and ripening the first year.

This interesting species is very rare in cultivation. Planted at Chevithorne Barton in 1993 from seed collected in Texas, it has been growing slowly but has made a healthy bush of about 50 cm tall and has proven to be hardy.

Quercus kelloggii Newb.

California black oak
California, Oregon

A large deciduous tree reaching 25 m or more in pine/oak forests on mountain slopes, this is the only oak in the Western United States that resembles eastern red oaks such as *Q. coccinea*. The leaves are broadly elliptic in outline, to 20 cm long and deeply cut into seven–eleven lobes, each of which ends in several bristle-tipped points. They are glossy deep green above, paler and nearly smooth beneath, or tomentose in forms from the south of the range that have been introduced recently. Acorns oblong to 4 cm long, ripening the second year and borne singly or in clusters of up to three on a short stalk.

In cultivation by 1873, it has reached 21 m at Tortworth Court, South Gloucestershire and Borde Hill, West Sussex.

It has grown slowly at Chevithorne Barton. Two trees planted in 1990 are now 4 m tall and are completely hardy.

Q. ×morehus Kellogg (*Q. kelloggii* × *Q. wislizeni*). A naturally occurring and variable hybrid found where the parents are found together. It is usually semi-evergreen with leaves resembling *Q. kelloggii* but more leathery and less deeply lobed. Some recent collections from a plant of the hybrid growing with *Q. kelloggii* closely resemble the latter. It has reached 12 m at Borde Hill, West Sussex. One planted here in 1998 has reached 3.5 m tall.

top left, right: *Q. kelloggii*
bottom left: *Q. ×morehus*

Quercus laevis Walter

Section *Lobate*

American turkey oak
SE United States

A medium-sized tree to 15 or sometimes 20 m tall, growing on poor sandy soils. The large leaves, to 20 or sometimes 30 cm long, are deeply cut into three–seven bristle-tipped lobes and are narrowed at the base to a short stalk only about 2 cm long. They are glossy green above, paler beneath, hairy when young, then becoming smooth, and are often held with the blade facing horizontally, no doubt an adaptation to avoid the intense sun in the areas where this species grows. The acorns are ovoid, about 3 cm long, and ripen the second year, borne singly or in pairs on a short stalk.

   Although introduced in 1823, this species grows poorly in this country and needs more heat to thrive. However, at Chevithorne Barton we have a fine young tree 3.5 m high, growing happily in a sheltered position in the Woodland Garden.

E Himalaya, N Myanmar, SW China

A striking tree, rare in cultivation, which reaches 35 m or more in the wild, occurring at altitudes of up to 2,800 m. Leaves very large to 30 cm or more long, with numerous parallel veins ending in small teeth, dark green above, glaucous beneath. Unusually for an oak, the buds are rounded. The acorns are almost hidden in large cups to 5 cm across, which are green and spongy when fresh but dry to resemble brown rosebuds with recurved scales.

Sir John Norton called it the finest of all oaks. Introduced in 1924 by the noted plant hunter George Forrest. It has reached 8 m at Caerhays, Cornwall. If it survives this will be an outstanding tree.

There are two specimens at Chevithorne Barton. One was given to us by the previous Chairman of the International Dendrology Society, Mr Carol Gurney, who said he could not make it grow in Suffolk. It is in a sheltered position south of the leat. It came through the 2005/06 winter unscathed, had good new growth in spring of 2007 and is now 2.5 m, having grown 1.5 m in two years. The second specimen, given to us by Hugh Cavendish, was obtained from Muncaster Castle, Cumbria. It is planted in the area known as North of the Tapir Orchard and has reached 1.3 m. It is healthy but a slow grower.

Quercus lancifolia Schltdl. & Cham.

Section *Lobatae*

S Mexico, C America

A large tree of 25 m or more in the tropical forests of its native habitat. Mature trees often have a buttressed base. Young shoots ridged, smooth. Leaves lanceolate to oblanceolate, to 12 cm long, taper-pointed at the tip and narrowed at the base to a short stalk. They are glossy dark green above and usually toothed above the middle, but entire towards the base. Acorns ovoid to 3 cm long, ripening the first year and borne singly or in pairs on a short stalk.

This species has proved delicate and difficult to grow at Chevithorne Barton. However, our two small trees came through the last two winters without serious frost damage and are now about 1.5 m tall. They have attractive red young foliage.

Quercus laurifolia Michx.

Laurel oak
SE United States

A fast-growing and large semi-evergreen tree to 30 m tall, sometimes more, with slender, smooth shoots. In the wild it can be found growing in moist and poorly drained soils. The usually unlobed leaves are up to 12 cm long, broadly elliptic to obovate, narrowed to a short stalk at the base and with a rounded tip. They are glossy green and more or less smooth on both sides. Acorns are ovoid to nearly rounded, about 1.5 cm long and ripen the second year. This species has been much confused with *Q. hemisphaerica*, but differs in the usually rounded tip to the leaf and the fact that it grows in a different habitat.

Introduced in 1786, it has reached 16 m at Glasnevin, Dublin.

The tree of this species here at Chevithorne Barton grew slowly at first but now appears well established and is about 8 m tall.

Quercus leucotrichophora A. Camus

Banj oak
Himalaya

An evergreen or semi-evergreen tree growing to 25 m or more in mountain forests where it is often associated with *Rhododendron arboreum*. Young shoots densely hairy. The leathery lanceolate leaves to 15 cm long are pointed at the tip, rounded at the base and edged with short, pointed teeth. They are silky hairy when young becoming dark green and smooth above, with a dense covering of white hairs beneath. Acorns ovoid to 2.5 cm long, ripening the second year, the appressed scales of the cup grey and hairy.

Introduced about 1815, it has reached 9 m at Dunloe Castle Hotel, Co. Kerry.

A tree planted at Chevithorne Barton in a sheltered position sustained some frost damage when young. It has grown well in the last two years and is now about 3 m tall. Plants received recently as *Q. lanata* seem to belong here. An attractive and exotic looking oak.

Q. tungmaiensis Y.T. Chang has been confused with *Q. lanata* and *Q. leucotrichophora* in China but has been shown to be a distinct species by Allen Coombes who identified our plant. In its native Tibet it makes a large deciduous tree with slender shoots densely covered in yellow-brown hairs. The oblong-lanceolate leaves can be up to 20 cm long with a sharply toothed margin and are glabrous beneath except on the veins. It was introduced by Keith Rushforth and grows at Tregrehan and here where it is a perfectly shaped small tree 2.5 m in height.

this page, top left and bottom; opposite page, top left:
Q. leucotrichophora
this page, top right; opposite page, bottom and right:
Q. tungmaiensis

Quercus libani G. Olivier

Lebanon oak
SW Asia

Usually a small deciduous tree to about 12 m tall, this species is closely related to *Q. castaneifolia* and grows in mountain forests with conifers and other oaks. The lance-shaped leaves are up to 10 cm long, glossy green above and usually smooth, or almost so, on both sides. They are pointed at the tip and edged with bristle-tipped teeth. The acorns are large and nearly rounded to cylindrical, to 3 cm long, ripening the second year with most of the acorn enclosed in a cup to 3.5 cm across, covered in appressed scales. They are borne singly or in pairs on a short, stout stalk.

Introduced about 1855, it has reached 26 m at Tortworth Court.

The largest of these oaks, planted at Chevithorne Barton in 1989, is now 8 m tall.

Quercus × libanerris Boom (*Q. cerris* × *Q. libani*). This vigorous hybrid occurs in Turkey, where the parents grow together but was first described from a tree at Arboretum Trompenburg. The lanceolate leaves to 13 cm long vary between those of the parent species. They are usually larger and more irregularly lobed than *Q. libani*. Acorns large, the cup with the scales of *Q. cerris* but shorter. This hybrid grows vigorously here. One, eighteen years old, is now 11.5 m tall and is a Champion Tree for the UK. Two selections have been made at Arboretum Trompenburg. 'Rotterdam' is closer to *Q. libani,* with regularly lobed leaves to 10 cm long and has reached 6 m here. 'Trompenburg' is closer to *Q. cerris*, with somewhat irregularly lobed leaves to 13 cm long and has reached 10 m. Both are vigorous young trees which seem to be growing at about a meter a year.

left, centre: *Q. libani*
top right, bottom right: *Q. ×libanerris*

Quercus lusitanica Lam

Section *Quercus*

S Spain, S Portugal, Morocco

A small evergreen shrub growing to 1 m tall, though often less, found on dry hills in oak and pine forests where it can often be seen creeping over rocky slopes. The leathery, obovate leaves to 5 cm long, or a little more, are short-stalked and edged with small, triangular teeth. They are hairy when young, becoming more or less smooth on both sides when mature. Acorns are ovoid and relatively large to 2.5 cm long, ripening the first year and usually borne singly on a short stalk. For many years this name was applied to *Q. faginea*.

Cultivated since before 1827, but surprisingly rare in cultivation.

There are three plants at Chevithorne Barton, the tallest 1 m.

Caucasus, N Iran

A vigorous and large deciduous tree forming forests in its native regions where it can reach 20 m or more in height. Young shoots stout, densely hairy, the buds with conspicuous slender, hairy stipules. Leaves obovate to 15 cm or more long and edged with rounded lobes. They are dark green above, paler beneath and densely covered, particularly on the underside, with velvety hairs. Acorns ovoid to 2.5 cm long, ripening the first year and borne singly or in small clusters. This species can hybridise with *Q. robur* and *Q. petraea* when grown from garden seed.

Introduced in 1873, it has reached 27 m at Westonbirt Arboretum.

At Chevithorne Barton we have two robust trees which seem acclimatised. The biggest one is 5.5 m high, the other 3.5 m.

Quercus macrocarpa Michx.

Bur oak, Mossy-cup oak, Prairie oak
E North America

A large deciduous tree in the wild reaching 40 m, this is a widely distributed and variable species found in a variety of habitats, from moist to dry soils and prairies, often on alkaline soils. The young shoots often have distinct corky ridges along their length. The large obovate leaves to 25 cm or more long are irregularly lobed but usually have a characteristic deep and broad sinus reaching almost to the midrib on both sides in the centre of the leaf. They are dark green above and pale blue-green beneath. The acorns are very variable in size. On trees in the south of the range they can be up to 5 cm long in a large cup conspicuously fringed with long bristles. Trees from further north perform better in this country but have smaller acorns in cups with a small fringe of bristles.

Introduced in 1811, it has reached 25 m in Holland Park, London.

The best specimen at Chevithorne Barton is 6 m tall.

Q. ×macdanielii T.L. Green & W.J. Hess (*Q. macrocarpa* × *Q. robur*). This hybrid was described from cultivation in the United States in 1998. It has smaller, shorter-stalked and less deeply lobed leaves than *Q. macrocarpa* and is expected to perform better here. We have one young specimen approximately 3 m high.

left, centre: *Q. macrocarpa*
right: *Q. ×macdanielii*

Quercus macrolepis Kotschy

Valonia oak
SE Europe, Turkey

A deciduous or semi-evergreen tree growing to 25 m in the wild where it occurs on mountain slopes and valleys associated with pines and other oaks. The ovate leaves are up to 15 cm long and are edged with prominent triangular bristle-tipped teeth. They are densely covered in grey hairs when young, becoming glossy dark green to grey-green above with a persistent covering of grey hairs beneath. Acorns ovoid to 5 cm long, ripening the second year and borne usually singly and unstalked in a large cup up to 5 cm across, densely covered in long, recurved woody scales.

Introduced in 1731, it has reached 22 m at Batsford Arboretum, Gloucestershire.

At Chevithorne Barton we have four specimens from a variety of sources. They are all growing well, if rather slowly. The biggest is about 6.5 m and has produced a few of the very distinctive acorns.

'Hemelrijk Silver' is a form with particularly large, silvery grey leaves. It was grown from seed collected on Rhodes by Robert and Jelena de Belder. We have two small plants of this selection, the taller one 2 m.

Q. brantii Lindl. This native of Southwest Asia is a small tree or large shrub. It differs from *Q. macropelis* in the more numerous and smaller teeth. Some plants under this name are close to *Q. libani* and may represent intermediates. We have two specimens, the biggest 2.5 m high.

left, centre: *Q. macrolepis* 'Hemelrijk Silver'
top right: *Q. brantii*
bottom right: *Q. macrolepis*

Quercus marilandica Münchh.

Blackjack oak
SE United States

A small, spreading deciduous tree to about 15 m tall, often found growing on poor, sandy soils. The very distinct, leathery leaves are up to 20 cm long, or more, and the same across. They are widest towards the end, where they are shallowly three-lobed with bristle-tipped teeth, untoothed and narrowed below the middle to a rounded base. When mature they are glossy dark green above with some yellowish hairs beneath. Acorns broadly ovoid to nearly rounded 2 cm long, ripening in two years, borne singly or in pairs on a very short stalk.

Introduced in the early 1700s, a more recent plant has reached 18 m at Leonardslee Gardens, West Sussex.

There is a small specimen here at Chevithorne Barton.

Q. ×bushii Sarg. (*Q. marilandica* × *Q. velutina*) A naturally occurring hybrid to 25 m tall, found where the parents grow together. This is a larger and faster-growing tree than *Q. marilandica*, with leaves intermediate between those of the parents. Some plants grown as *Q. marilandica* prove to be this hybrid. It has reached 4 m here.

left: *Q. marilandica*
centre, right: *Q. ×bushii*

Mexico

A semi-evergreen tree widely distributed in Mexico, where it is found mainly in oak/pine forests above 2,000 m and makes a spreading tree to about 15 m or more tall. The leathery oblong leaves to 10 cm long are untoothed with a pointed or blunt tip. They are dark green above, paler beneath and covered with hairs when young, becoming more or less smooth when mature. Acorns ovoid to 1.5 cm long, ripening the second year and borne singly or in pairs. In Mexico the leaves turn red-purple before they fall in late winter.

The first introduction of this species seems to be that of Michael Frankis, who collected it in Nuevo León, northern Mexico, in 1992. It has proved very fast growing and hardy in cultivation, and has reached 12 m at Hillier Gardens.

We have three specimens at Chevithorne Barton. The two older ones have grown very fast and straight to 9 and 11 m. This oak has very distinctive bark and seems entirely hardy.

Q. miquihuanensis Nixon & C.H. Mull.

Section *Lobatae*

NE Mexico

A dense evergreen shrub reaching 2 or sometimes 3 m in its native regions, where it grows in the mountains in scrub or pine/oak forests. The thickly leathery elliptic to obovate leaves are up to 5 cm long and 2 cm wide and are dark green above with deeply impressed veins and have a dense covering of rusty brown hairs beneath, which falls or rubs off with age. The margins are entire except for a short point at the tip or with few small teeth and are distinctly revolute. Acorns ovoid to 1.5 cm long, borne singly or in pairs on a short stout stalk, ripening the second year. This species has a restricted distribution and is listed as Endangered in the Red List of Oaks.

This very distinct species was only described in 1993. It was introduced recently by Nick Macer of Pan-Global Plants, who was, with Allen Coombes, the first to positively identify it at an oak weekend at Chevithorne Barton in September 2007.

It seems to tolerate the variable Devon climate but looks as if it needs more sun, so we intend to move it to the sunniest position we can find. We also have young plants of the closely related *Q. hintoniorum* Nixon & C.H. Mull., another recent introduction. Allen Coombes introduced a similar, as yet unnamed, species from Oaxaca in 2008.

Quercus monimotricha Hand.-Mazz.

Section *Cerris*

SW China, N Myanmar

This species is one of a group about twelve Chinese golden oaks, all except one of which come from China and surrounding areas. A dense and slow-growing evergreen shrub with downy shoots, reaching about 3 m. Its leaves are ovate to 4 cm long, short-stalked and edged with sharp spiny teeth, rough above, green to grey-green and softly downy beneath. Acorns are borne in short-stalked clusters among the foliage, ripening the second year.

From the plants raised at the Hillier Gardens, it would appear to come true from garden seed. It is also one of the few shrubby, suckering oaks. In its native habitat it forms extensive carpets at high altitudes.

Introduced from Yunnan by the noted plant collector Roy Lancaster in 1986, it has reached 1.2 x 2 m at the Hillier Gardens.

The plant at Chevithorne Barton was acquired from the Hillier Gardens in 2003 and is descended from Lancaster's original collection. It is not growing in conditions in which it would naturally be found, but seems to be doing very healthily on a bank near the herbaceous borders. It has a very small leaf, has made a low, compact bush 30 cm high and flowers well. A second plant has been set in the ground nearby in the hope of producing acorns. They both seem to be completely hardy. Unusually for an oak, flowers can be produced from an early age and have been seen on plants less than two years old from seed. However, not all plants in cultivation appear to produce fruit freely. An interesting oak for the smaller garden.

C & S China

An evergreen tree with a rounded head growing to 12 m tall and found in mountain woodlands above 1,000 m. The oblong to lance-shaped leaves up to 15 cm long are tapered to a fine point at the tip and rounded at the base, the numerous veins ending in small, pointed teeth. They are glossy green and smooth above when mature and glaucous beneath with white hairs. Acorns ovoid to 1.8 cm long, ripening the second year, and borne singly or in clusters of up to five fruits on a short stalk. The cup is thin and bears scales in six–seven concentric rings. Plants propagated from a tree at Arboretum des Barres in France, originally called *Q. oxyodon* and later *Q. liboensis*, are close to this species but the fruits ripen the first year.

Introduced from Hunan, southern China, by Allen Coombes in 2004 but certainly in cultivation before this as seed has been available from the Shanghai Botanic Garden for some time.

At Chevithorne Barton we have two small plants from a recent introduction, one of which has come through the winter very satisfactorily.

Quercus myrsinifolia Blume

Subgenus Cyclobalanopsis

Japan, S Korea, China

A rounded evergreen tree to 15 m tall, sometimes shrubby with several stems from the base. The slender, glabrous shoots bear lanceolate leaves to 10 cm long ending in a long, tapered point and shallowly toothed above the middle. They emerge bronze when young becoming glossy dark green above and blue-green and glabrous beneath. Acorns ovoid to 2.5 cm long, ripening the first year, with several arranged on a stalk to 5 cm long, the cup with seven–nine concentric scales.

This very hardy species performs better in this country than any other member of the subgenus Cyclobalanopsis. Although sometimes regarded as synonymous with *Q. glauca*, it is quite distinct. The young foliage emerges late in spring and escapes damage by late frosts.

Introduced by the noted plant collector Robert Fortune in 1854, it has reached 11 m in the grounds of South Lodge Hotel, Horsham, West Sussex.

We have three of these trees at Chevithorne Barton, which tend to be multi-stemmed. The biggest of them is about 6 m high and 6 m across and makes a very fine and rounded tree.

Q. glauca Thunb. The Japanese blue oak, or Ring-cupped oak, is sometimes confused with *Q. myrsinifolia* but differs in its broader leaves, hairy beneath. Sadly its attractive, bronze new growth emerges very early in the year and can then be damaged by spring frosts, but it is worth growing for its young foliage alone. Widely distributed in East Asia, it was introduced in 1804 and has reached 16 m at Borde Hill. Some plants obtained here under this name have proved to be *Q. myrsinifolia*, but the true species is now represented by small plants in our nursery.

Q. schottkyana Rehder & E.H. Wilson is a close relative of *Q. glauca* from southwest China and differs in its densely white-hairy, often pink-flushed, young foliage. Introduced to

Kew in 1992. This oak has grown well here and one tree is about 10 m high, making it the biggest of the Chinese introductions. It seems hardy and is well worth growing.

top left, bottom left: *Q. myrsinifolia*
centre top, centre bottom, right: *Q. schottkyana*

Quercus nigra L.

Water oak
SE United States

A distinctive semi-evergreen tree of up to about 25 m which comes from the Southeastern United States, where it tends to grow in valley bottoms. Leaves often crowded at the end of short twigs, extremely variable in shape, mostly obovate, some with shallow and deep lobes towards the apex, often long and narrow on young trees but becoming smaller with age. Leaves are pale green and glabrous on both sides and often remain on the tree until spring.

Introduced in 1723, it has reached 19 m at Windsor Great Park.

Two trees planted at Chevithorne Barton in 1990 have grown into substantial multi-stemmed trees of 9 m and 11 m. They seem perfectly hardy but take a lot of pruning to keep them in good shape. Some leaves on some trees turn a good yellow in autumn. It is closely related to *Q. laurifolia*, *Q. phellos* and *Q. hemisphaerica*. A worthwhile tree which should have a place in any collection.

Himalaya, China

An evergreen tree reaching 20 m tall in the wild, where it is found in mountain forests. The leathery ovate to lanceolate leaves are up to 20 cm long and end in a long, tapered point. They are bronze and silky hairy when young, becoming smooth and glossy dark green above, blue-green beneath, the numerous veins ending in short pointed teeth. Acorns ovoid to nearly rounded to 2 cm long, ripening the first year and borne singly or in small clusters on stalks to 5 cm long. The cup bears six–eight toothed concentric scales.

Introduced by the notable plant collector Ernest 'Chinese' Wilson in 1900, it has reached 10 m at Caerhays, Cornwall. An introduction from Guizhou, China, is 8 m at Hillier Gardens twelve years after planting.

This oak grows well at Chevithorne Barton, where the tallest, planted in 1998, is over 3.5 m. The leaves persist through the winter and it is one of the best Chinese oaks that we have grown.

Quercus pacifica Nixon & C.H. Mull.

Channel Islands scrub oak
California islands

An evergreen or semi-evergreen shrub or small tree growing to 5 m tall or more, and found in hillside scrub. The obovate leaves to 4 cm long are narrowed to the base and rounded at the tip, either entire or with a few spiny teeth, although on juvenile plants leaves tend to be rounded at the base and more spiny. They are glossy green and smooth above, paler with sparse hairs beneath. The conical acorns taper to a point at the tip and ripen the first year, borne singly or in pairs. It is listed as Vulnerable in the Red List of Oaks.

Only described in 1994, this species was introduced to the UK by Allen Coombes in 1997 following the 2nd International Oak Conference in California. It has reached 1 m here.

We have two plants of this species at Chevithorne Barton: both small bushes, the largest 60–70 cm tall. It grows very slowly but appears completely hardy: rather surprising as it comes from frost-free areas. The following related species are also growing well here as young plants.

Q. berberidifolia Liebm. California scrub oak. This widespread species from California and Baja California, in Mexico, where it grows on dry slopes and in oak and pine woodland, makes a shrub or small tree to 4 m tall. It differs from *Q. pacifica* in the blunt-tipped acorns and the smaller spinier leaves, usually rounded at the base.

Q. dumosa Nutt. Nuttall scrub oak. A species with a restricted distribution in coastal hills and scrub in Southern California and Baja California. It makes a shrub to 2.5 m tall with small spiny leaves to 2.5 cm long, glossy green above and covered with grey hairs beneath. It is listed as Endangered in the Red List of Oaks. Most plants originally grown under this name were probably the more widely distributed *Q. berberidifolia*.

Q. durata Jeps. Leather oak. An evergreen shrub to 2 m tall with rigid spiny leaves to 4 cm long, grey-green above and hairy on both sides. The acorns are blunt-tipped. Found in California on serpentine soils.

left: *Q. durata*
top centre: *Q. pacifica*
bottom centre: *Q. berberidifolia*
right: *Q. dumosa*

Quercus palustris Münchh.

Pin oak
E United States

A fast-growing, deciduous tree to 25 m or more in the wild, where it is found in moist or poorly drained soils. It has a characteristic conical crown, the lower branches often drooping. The leaves are elliptic to obovate in outline but are deeply cut into five–nine lobes, each one ending in several bristle-tipped teeth. They are glossy dark green above, paler and glossy beneath, with conspicuous tufts of hair in the vein axils. Autumn colour is red. Acorns nearly rounded to 1.5 cm long, ripening the second year and borne singly or in short-stalked clusters of two or three.

Introduced in 1800, it has reached 28 m in Hyde Park, London.

This was one of the first trees planted in the collection here, at Chevithorne Barton. It is now of classic shape, 20 m tall, and usually colours well in autumn.

Q. ×schochiana Dieck (*Q. palustris* × *Q. phellos*). A naturally occurring hybrid found where the parents grow together, it has narrow leaves with few pointed lobes. In cultivation since at least 1894, it has reached 17 m at Winkworth Arboretum, Surrey. There is a young tree here, about 8 m tall. Some plants distributed under this name are *Q.* 'Souvenir de Jacques Lombarts'.

left: *Q. palustris* 'Silhouette'
bottom left: *Q. palustris*
bottom centre: *Q. palustris* 'Compacta'
right: *Q.* 'Souvenir de Jacques Lombarts'

Quercus petraea (Matt.) Liebl.

Section Quercus

Sessile oak, Durmast oak
Europe, N Turkey, Caucasus

A large deciduous tree to 40 m tall, often dominant in forests or growing with other oaks. The broadly elliptic to obovate leaves, to 15 cm long, are with six–eight shallow rounded lobes on each side and are borne on a distinct stalk to 4 cm long. They are dark green and slightly glossy above, blue-green with some hairs beneath. Acorns are ovoid to 4 cm long, ripening the first year and borne singly or in small clusters, unstalked or with a very short stalk.

A British native, widely distributed but most common in the north and west, this species can be distinguished from the more frequently seen *Q. robur* by the long-stalked leaves and the unstalked acorns.

It has reached 40 m at Knole Park, Kent.

At Chevithorne Barton we do not have big established trees of this species but eight cultivars are represented here, of which two are particularly interesting. 'Laciniata Crispa' is an unusual form originally introduced from Germany in 1928, with slender thread-like hanging leaves. It is 6.5 m here. 'Purpurea', also introduced from Germany in about 1865, is a slow-growing selection with purple leaves, 2.5 m tall. We have good examples of both these oaks here, as well as of the two below.

Q. hartwissiana Steven (*Q. stranjensis* Turrill.) This relative of *Q. petraea* from Bulgaria, Turkey and the Caucasus has large obovate leaves to 20 cm long with up to twelve shallow lobes on each side. The petiole is long, as in *Q. petraea*, but the acorns are on stalks to 8 cm long as in *Q. robur*. It has reached 15 m at Hillier Gardens. Here it has made a good-shaped tree of 4 m tall.

.

Q. ×streimii Heuff. (*Q. petraea × Q. pubescens*). This hybrid can be found in southern Europe where the parent species grow together. We have small plants of 'Kortrijk' with deeply cut leaves and 'Lanze' with lanceolate wavy-edged leaves.

top left: *Q. ×streimii*
bottom left: *Q. hartwissiana*
right: *Q. petraea* 'Lanciniata Crispa'

Willow oak
E United States

One of the red oaks, this is normally a large tree with slender hairless twigs which are olive-brown in colour when young. The bark is smooth and grey on young plants, later becoming darker and forming irregular rough ridges and furrows. Leaves are between 5 and 12 cm long, pale green, willow-like in shape with an entire margin, and turn yellow and orange in autumn, some often persisting into winter. Acorns mature over two years and are very small, from 0.5 to 1 cm across, nearly round and much beloved by squirrels.

This is an attractive and hardy tree which can grow to a considerable size – up to 25 m, in its preferred habitat. Originating from the Eastern United States, this is a species from the swamp margins and it thrives in damp conditions, although it will also manage quite well in dry sandy soils.

Introduced to Europe in 1723, it has reached 24 m at Kew.

There are three specimens at Chevithorne Barton. Two were planted in 1990 and are compact and rather bushy trees, about 3.5 m high. Both of these were planted in the area known as North of the Tapir Orchard. The third was planted more recently and is 4 m high and growing well. This species appears hardy in our climate. Its natural inclination is to form a neat, round shaped crown, so very little pruning has been required so far. However, it is reported that when left to their own devices, lower branches do not readily self-prune. In autumn, the leaves can colour handsomely: a rich buttery yellow, shrimp-pink and orange. This species is often planted as a street tree in North America, but here in Europe it is rarely used by landscapers, which is a shame because apart from its hardiness, the Willow Oak has much to offer in terms of colour, shape and manageability.

'Latifolia' is a selection described in 1838 with larger, toothed leaves. It is of hybrid origin and has reached 4 m in height.

Q. ×heterophylla F. Michx. (*Q. phellos* × *Q. rubra*). This naturally occurring hybrid can be found where the parents grow together. In cultivation it is a fast-growing spreading tree with oblong to elliptic leaves to 15 cm long which vary from being entire to having several pointed teeth or lobes on each side. The leaves can turn red to red-brown in autumn. In cultivation by 1822, it has reached 22 m at Glasnevin, Dublin. We have two good trees here, the taller one 6 m high.

top left: *Q. phellos* 'Latifolia'
bottom left, centre: *Q. phellos*
top right, top far right, bottom right: *Q. ×heterophylla*

Quercus phillyreoides A. Gray

Section *Cerris*

Japan, China, Korea

A very distinct and hardy evergreen tree of bushy, spreading or upright habit, sometimes a shrub, growing up to 15 m tall. The short-stalked leathery leaves are ovate to obovate with small blunt teeth above the middle and up to 6 cm long on downy shoots. They are bronze when young becoming glossy dark green above, paler and glossy beneath and nearly smooth on both sides. Acorns ovoid to 2 cm long, ripening the second year, borne singly or in pairs on a stalk to 4 cm long. The specific epithet derives from the resemblance of the foliage to that of *Phillyrea latifolia*.

Introduced in 1861, it has reached 10 m at Caerhays, Cornwall.

Here at Chevithorne Barton, as well as one free-standing tree of about 5 m tall, we have this species planted both as a hedge and as a large and dense clipped bush.

W Mexico

A spreading tree reaching up to 20 m tall in its native country, where it grows on well-drained, often sandy soils in tropical, semi-deciduous woodland. The young shoots are densely covered with yellowish hairs, becoming more or less smooth with age. The leathery obovate leaves are up to 22 cm long, dark green above, paler beneath and edged with bristly teeth, or rarely entire. Acorns ripening the first year to about 2 cm long, borne singly in an unstalked flat cup up to 3 cm wide.

Introduced in 1995 by Allen Coombes from Nayarit, Mexico.

We are very pleased to have two trees of this rare species from the original introduction here at Chevithorne Barton. They took some time to become established, but are now 3.5 m tall and are growing well.

Quercus polymorpha Schltdl. & Cham.

Section *Quercus*

Netleaf white oak
Texas, Mexico, Guatemala

A semi-evergreen tree to 20 m tall which, although widely distributed in Mexico, was found only as late as 1992 as a small population in Texas. The leaves, as the name suggests, are very variable in shape from ovate to oblong or obovate, up to 15 cm long and either entire or toothed above the middle. They are rounded or heart-shaped at the base and often on a long stalk. Bronze-red and hairy when young, they become green to blue-green above and grey-green beneath. Acorns ovoid to 2.5 cm long, densely downy when young, ripening the first year. It is listed as Near Threatened in the Red List of Oaks.

Grown in Britain since at least 1996, when it was introduced by Allen Coombes, from near Monterrey, Nuevo León, where it grows with *Q. rysophylla*. It performs best in areas with hot summers.

We have two trees that are established at Chevithorne Barton, the largest of which is about 3 m tall and appears hardy.

Armenian oak
NE Turkey, Georgia

A very distinctive small tree, or medium-sized to large shrub, with stout shoots and large winter buds. The deciduous leaves are large, oval to obovate, sometimes as much as 25 cm long and 12 cm wide, strongly ribbed and toothed with a yellow petiole and midrib. Long pendulous male catkins are a feature in spring. Acorns are ovoid or rounded on short stout stalks. In its native habitat it spreads by self layering. It has a restricted distribution in the wild and is listed as Vulnerable in the Red List of Oaks.

Introduced into Germany in 1885, and to the UK probably in 1905 by Lord Kesteven (Henry Elwes). It has reached 10 m at Hidcote, Gloucestershire.

A striking and unmistakable species, it grows slowly but is known to have viable acorns when quite young. It first fruited at Chevithorne Barton in 2006. It often has rich yellow autumn colour. Here, one planted in 2002 in the Rifle Range is a vigorous dome-shaped bush of about 2.5 m and seems hardy. A second one, in a sheltered spot in the area known as North of the Tapir Orchard, is proving a very slow grower. One of the best oaks to grow in the UK, especially in a smaller garden.

It is a parent of the well-known and worthwhile hybrid, *Q.* Pondaim Group (*Q. pontica* × *Q. dentata*). We have an established tree of this hybrid of 5 m tall.

Q. ×*hickelii* A. Camus (*Q. pontica* × *Q. robur*). This hybrid can occur when *Q. pontica* is raised from garden seed. It generally makes a small tree branching low down and has reached 13 m at the Royal Botanic Garden, Edinburgh. It is 9 m high here.

Q. sadleriana R.Br. ter. The Deer oak is a small evergreen or semi-evergreen shrub from California and Oregon, close to *Q. pontica*, but has smaller, though longer-stalked, leaves with fewer veins and smaller acorns. We have three small plants here.

top, bottom: *Q. pontica*

left, centre: *Q. xhickelii*
right: *Q. sadleriana*

Quercus pyrenaica Willd.

Pyrenean oak
SW Europe, Morocco

A deciduous tree growing to about 25 m in the wild, more rarely shrubby, with densely tomentose shoots. Leaves more or less elliptic in outline, to 20 cm long, and cut, usually deeply, into four–seven lobes on each side, the lobes sometimes with few rounded teeth. They emerge late in the year, densely covered in white hairs, becoming dark green above, grey-green and hairy beneath. Acorns to 4 cm long, ripening the first year and borne in clusters of up to four on a stalk to 5 cm long.

Introduced in 1822, it has reached 24 m at Melbury Park, Dorset. It is one of the last deciduous oaks to come into leaf and flower.

'Pendula', described in 1879, is the most commonly grown form, with weeping branches. It has reached 25 m at Bicton Park, East Devon. We have a well established tree about 6 m high and 10 m in width.

left, right: *Q. pyrenaica* 'Pendula'

Quercus robur L.

English oak, Pedunculate oak
Europe, Caucasus

This magnificent, large, deciduous tree is the
only native oak found here at Chevithorne
Barton and is represented by many trees.
In its typical form it is widely distributed
throughout Britain and Europe, reaching the
Caucasus mountains. Several geographical
variants are recognised in Eastern Europe and
West Asia. The obovate dark green leaves,
smooth and blue-green beneath, are up to 10
cm long or more and usually have five–seven
shallow rounded lobes on each side. They are
borne on a short stalk of less than 1 cm and
have small auricles at the base. Acorns ovoid
to 4 cm long and ripening the first year,
usually several borne on a stalk to 12 cm long.

It has reached 40 m at Stourhead,
Wiltshire. We have many distinctive
geographical variants and cultivars in the
collection (too many to describe here),
which are doing well. Our climate here
seems to suit them.

Q. robur Fastigiata Group, known as
the Cypress oak, includes trees and cultivars
with generally upright branches. 'Pectinata',
an old cultivar from Germany, has finely cut
leaves and has attained 18 m in East Lothian,
Scotland. *Q. robur* Pendula Group, another
old form, has drooping shoots.

left: *Q. robur* 'Filicifolia'
right: *Q. robur*

Quercus rubra L.

Red oak
E North America

This fast-growing and large deciduous tree is the most commonly grown species of its group in this country and can reach 30 m or more. The leaves are up to 20 cm or more long with three–five rather shallow lobes on each side and are borne on a usually red-flushed petiole. Each lobe is further divided, ending in bristle-tipped teeth. They are dark dull green above, blue-green beneath and usually turn yellow-brown in autumn. Acorns ovoid to 3 cm long in a shallow cup, ripening the second year.

Introduced in the early 1700s, it has reached 32 m at Crowsley Park, Oxfordshire.

We have four oaks of this species at Chevithorne Barton, where they grow well, the tallest being about 12 m.

Q. rubra Aurea Group, has golden yellow young foliage turning green after mid-summer. It has reached 22 m in Stirling, Scotland. The leaves are a dramatic buttery yellow here when they emerge, mostly turning greener as the year progresses. 'Cyrille', named by Allen Coombes in 2002, was originally grown as *Q. ×fernaldii* (*Q. ilicifolia* × *Q. rubra*). Its leaves are very variable, from narrow with long bristles to almost normal, but with distinct reticulate yellow-green veins caused by a virus. We also have the recently introduced multi-coloured 'Magic Fire'.

left, centre top: *Q. rubra*
centre bottom, right: *Q. rubra* Aurea Group

Netleaf oak
SW United States, Mexico, Guatemala

A large and widely distributed evergreen tree growing up to 30 m tall and found in mountain forests. The hard leathery short-stalked leaves, to 20 cm long, are ovate to obovate and usually distinctly convex and unlobed but with a few small teeth on the margin. They emerge covered in red hairs, becoming glossy dark green and smooth above, blue-green to glaucous and slightly hairy beneath. Acorns ovoid, variable in size, to 2.5 cm long, ripening the first year, several to many borne on a long stalk to 10 cm or more.

Introduced in 1839 but rare in cultivation, it has reached 9 m at the Hillier Gardens.

This is one of the white oaks at Chevithorne Barton which we have had difficulty getting established, but one tree about two years old has finally got going, is now 2.5 m high and looks very healthy.

Q. obtusata × Q. rugosa is the suspected parentage of plants introduced from Mexico in 1999. A plant here has less convex leaves than *Q. rugosa* and one plant produced very good autumn colour in 2007. This hybrid, although very delicate, produces very striking leaves. Our two plants have struggled to get going but in the last two years have become established – the tallest is now about 1.5 m high.

Q. peduncularis Née This species is a smaller tree than *Q. rugosa*, with densely hairy shoots and oblanceolate to obovate leaves with up to nine shallow rounded lobes on each side. Up to five acorns are borne on a stalk to 15 cm long. Introduced from Jalisco, Mexico, by Allen Coombes in 1995. This species, although very delicate, produces very striking leaves and now finally looks at least partially established. It is probably the only one in the country.

Q. subspathulata Trel. A large tree to 25 m in the wild, this species has obovate leaves that are entire or edged with shallow rounded lobes. Up to three acorns are borne at the end of a stalk to 10 cm long. Introduced from Michoacán, Mexico, by Allen Coombes in 1995, it is listed as Vulnerable in the Red List of Oaks. Another delicate oak which has not adapted well to our climate.

top left: *Q. rugosa*
bottom left: *Q. peduncularis*
top centre, top right: *Q. obtusata × Q. rugosa*
bottom centre: *Q. obtusata × Q. rugosa*
bottom right: *Q. subspathulata*

Quercus rysophylla Weath.

Monterrey oak, Loquat oak
E Mexico

A strong-growing evergreen tree to 20 m or more in the wild. Bark smooth and grey on young trees, becoming dark and rough, cracked into chunky pale grey blocks. Young shoots prominently ridged. Leaves large, elliptic, to 25 cm long, lobed and toothed on young trees and vigorous shoots, entire or nearly so on mature trees, often red or bronze when young, becoming glossy dark green with deeply impressed veins. Acorns on a very short stalk, ovoid, with a pointed tip, 1–1.7 cm long and ripening the second year.

Its natural habitat is warm, temperate pine-oak woodland between 400 and 2,100 m, and it often occurs on north-facing slopes. It is listed as Near Threatened in the Red List of Oaks.

Here at Chevithorne Barton, our tallest tree has achieved 12 m and seems hardy. It has a good shape and grows fast. We have another tree from a collection Allen Coombes made in 1996, at the Horsetail Falls (Cascada Cola de Caballo) near Monterrey, Mexico, at an altitude of 1,250 m.

There is a fine specimen of 17 m (in 2007) with a slightly different leaf at Hillier Gardens, which is still growing vigorously.

John Grimshaw of Cheltenham, Gloucestershire, thinks it is possibly the best introduction of a hardwood tree since the Second World War. It is certainly a distinctive, well-shaped, fairly hardy tree which fits well into an English setting. Acorns are occasionally produced in cultivation: these, however, mainly give hybrids with other red oaks.

First introduced to Hillier Gardens in 1978, it was also collected Sir Harold Hillier the following year from a spot above the Horsetail Falls by.

Quercus salicina Blume

Subgenus *Cyclobalanopsis*

S Japan, S Korea

A relative of *Quercus glauca*, this is a rare evergreen tree, usually less than 12 m tall in its natural habitat of South Korea and southern Japan, and probably smaller in the UK. Bark is dark greyish black and smooth. Glossy green leaves have prominent secondary veins (six to thirteen) on each side of the mid-vein and feel papery or leathery. Leaves up to 15 cm long, narrow lanceolate, taper-pointed, with sharp serrations on the upper half of the margin, glaucous beneath. Young growth bronze to deep bronze-purple. The tree flowers in July or August, and fruits the following year between August and November.

Introduced in about 1895, it has reached 8 m at the Hillier Gardens.

This oak has a reputation of being difficult to establish. However, there are two specimens at Chevithorne Barton, both flourishing and apparently completely hardy. They do, however, need a sheltered spot and a lot of pruning and thinning to keep them in good shape. They were planted in 1990 and have developed into small multi-stemmed trees, the larger about 8 m tall. Consequently they are among the most worthwhile of the willow-type oaks to grow in the UK, and worth trying if only for the dramatic colour of the young growth, which is particularly striking in one of the trees here.

Q. stenophylloides Hayata, from Taiwan, is closely related. It has lance-shaped leaves, glaucous beneath and edged with sharp teeth. Introduced to the Royal Botanic Garden, Edinburgh in 1993, and by Allen Coombes in 2003. This oak has survived two winters here, so may well be established.

top left, bottom left: *Q. salicina*
centre, top right, bottom right: *Q. stenophylloides*

Quercus sapotifolia Liebm.

S Mexico, C America

A large and widely distributed evergreen tree to 30 m or more in the wild, found growing in humid forests in tropical regions as far south as Panama. Leaves unlobed, elliptic to oblanceolate, to 12 cm long, usually rounded at the tip and narrowed at the base to a short stalk. They emerge red when young, becoming glossy dark green above. Acorns ovoid to 1.5 cm long, ripening the first year.

Introduced from Oaxaca, Mexico, by Allen Coombes in 1997. For the hybrid with *Q. castanea*, see under that species.

Another delicate oak which has done much better in the last two years and is now 2.5 m high. It is probably the only one in the country.

Mexico

A vigorous semi-evergreen tree growing to 20 m or more in Mexico, where it is widely distributed and variable. Leaves lanceolate, to 25 cm long or more, tapered to a long slender point at the tip, narrowed or rounded at the base and on a petiole to 5 cm long. They are edged with up to twelve bristle-tipped teeth on each side. Emerging covered in red hairs when young, they become glossy green above. Acorns ovoid to 1.5 cm long, borne singly or in small clusters, ripening the first year.

Most of the older plants in cultivation derive from introductions by Allen Coombes – from Puebla in 1995 and from San Luis Potosi the following year, but plants from an independent introduction were distributed in 1994. We have four established trees at Chevithorne Barton, the tallest at 8 m. This oak does well in Devon.

Quercus semecarpifolia Sm.

Section *Cerris*

Himalaya, Tibet

A remarkable, large, very hardy evergreen tree reaching 30 m in its native habitat, where it grows in oak/pine forests at high altitudes. It has stout shoots, downy when young. Short-stalked leathery leaves, to 10 cm long, ovate to oblong and untoothed, but edged with spiny teeth on young plants and juvenile shoots. They are glossy dark green above and densely covered with yellow-brown hairs beneath when young, becoming green. Acorns rounded to 2.5 cm long, ripening the second year and borne stalkless or on short stalks, singly or in pairs. This is the best known of a group of closely related species, which are often confused.

Introduced in 1894 by C. Gilbert Rogers and in 1900 by James S. Gamble, both of the Dehra Dun Forestry School, India. A tree from the earlier collection has reached 21 m at Tregrehan, Cornwall. We have three established trees at Chevithorne Barton, now growing well. The tallest is about 3.5 m.

Q. guajavifolia H. Lév. Southwest China. A tree to 15 m tall, sometimes shrubby, the leaves brown, tomen-tose beneath. Acorns borne on a stalk to 6 cm long and with a characteristic wavy-edged cup. We have just planted the first specimen out in its final position and it seems to have come through the winter unscathed.

Q. longispica (Hand.-Mazz.) A. Camus. Southwest China. This species is distinct in having the acorns borne along long stalks to 15 cm. The leaves are oblong to obovate, to 8 cm long, entire or nearly so, but spine-toothed on juvenile plants with a yellow tomentum beneath. Introduced by Roy Lancaster in 1981, it has reached 7 m at the Hillier Gardens. We have a small one in the collection.

Q. pseudosemecarpifolia A. Camus. A tree to 20 m or more, this species has leaves that are glossy green on both sides, emerging bronze when young. We have two good young trees here and a third planted in 2003. Upright and hardy, the taller plant is about 3.5 m.

top left, bottom left: *Q. semecarpifolia*
top centre, bottom centre: *Q. guajavifolia*
top right: *Q. longispica*
bottom right: *Q. pseudosemecarpifolia*

Quercus serrata Thunb.

Section *Quercus*

Q. glandulifera Blume
Japan, Korea, China

A deciduous, medium-sized tree reaching 15 m or, more rarely, 25 m, found in mixed forests in mountain regions. The young shoots are silky hairy when they emerge, becoming smooth with age. Leaves obovate to 18 cm long, edged with small forward-pointing teeth, tapered at the apex and narrowed to a petiole to 3 cm long (very short in *Q. serrata* var. *brevipetiolata* (DC.) Nakai). They emerge silky hairy and often pinkish, becoming dark green above and grey-green with persistent hairs beneath, turning red in autumn, some leaves often remaining green into winter. Acorns ovoid to 2.5 cm long, ripening the first year and borne singly or in small clusters on a short stalk. It can hybridise with *Q. robur* when grown from garden seed.

Introduced by Charles Sargent in 1893, it has reached 17 m at Tregrehan, Cornwall.

We have three good trees at Chevithorne Barton, the biggest about 5.5 m.

Shumard oak
E United States

A large, spreading, deciduous tree growing to 25 m or more. Mostly found in lowland areas, often in poorly drained soils, by swamps or streams. The long-stalked, elliptic to obovate, leaves are up to 20 cm long and deeply cut usually into seven–nine lobes, which themselves are divided and end in bristle-tipped teeth. They are glossy dark green above, paler and glossy beneath, with conspicuous tufts of white hairs in the axils of the veins. Autumn colour is usually late and often a good deep red. Acorns ovoid to nearly rounded, to 3 cm long, ripening the second year.

Introduced in 1897, it has reached 20 m at Kew.

We have three established trees of this species, two of which are about 7 m high. In addition we have a fine specimen grown from an acorn which I collected in Kentucky about twenty years ago, and which is now 9 m high.

Q. acerifolia (E.J. Palmer) Stoynoff & Hess (*Q. shumardii* var. *acerifolia* E.J. Palmer). Maple-leaf oak. This rare relative of *Q. shumardii* makes a smaller tree to 15 m tall. The leaves are shorter and almost as broad as long, suggesting the shape of those of the sugar maple, *Acer saccharum*. Although rare in cultivation, it makes an excellent oak for the smaller garden giving good autumn colour. It is only found in a few localities in Arkansas and is listed as Endangered in the Red List of Oaks. Introduced to the Hillier Gardens in 1989, where it has reached 6 m.

Q. buckleyi Nixon & Dorr. Buckley oak. Differing from *Q. shumardii* in its smaller size and smaller leaves with inconspicuous tufts of hair on the underside, this species is native to Texas and Oklahoma where it can be found on limestone soils. It has been referred to in the past as *Q. texana* and has reached 9 m at Hillier Gardens. We have good young specimens of both these two last species in the collection.

top, bottom: *Q. shumardii*

left, centre: *Q. acerifolia*
right: *Q. buckleyi*

Quercus texana Buckley

Q. nuttallii E.J. Palmer
Texas red oak, Nuttall oak
SE United States

A deciduous tree to 25 m or more in the wild, where it grows in moist, low lying river valleys. It is close to *Q. palustris*, differing in usually larger leaves with more lobes and with larger acorns in a deeper cup. Leaves elliptic in outline, to 20 cm long on a smooth stalk to 5 cm, deeply cut with up to eleven lobes that are further divided, ending in bristle-tipped teeth. Often bronze when young in summer, they are dark green above when mature, with conspicuous tufts of white hairs in the axils of the underside of the leaves. Autumn colour is late and deep red. Acorns ovoid to oblong, to 3 cm long, ripening the second year and borne singly or in pairs and stalkless or almost so. In spite of its name it is only found in a small part of eastern Texas.

This species is often known under its incorrect synonym *Q. nuttallii*. It has reached 17 m at Glasnevin, Dublin.

First planted at Chevithorne Barton in 1992. There are four trees, the tallest 6 m. This species grows well here, often going a good colour in autumn, and is hardy.

Q. texana New Madrid Group is a striking seed selection from Guy Sternberg with deep red-purple young foliage. Our tree, probably a clone of the Group, is about 2 m high.

Quercus trojana Webb.

Macedonian oak
SE Europe, W Turkey

A medium-sized, late deciduous tree, to
20 m tall, found in oak and pine forests in
the wild. It is often upright in habit, at least
when young, with downy young shoots.
The short-stalked leaves are oblong to ovate,
to 10 cm long, with a pointed tip and are
edged with small teeth. They are hairy on
both sides when young, becoming glossy
dark green above, paler beneath, and remain
green until late in the year. Acorns ovoid to
nearly rounded to 4 cm long, ripening the
second year in a sessile or very short-stalked
cup. A plant received as *Q. ×hispanica*
'Hemelrijk' belongs here.

Introduced in 1890, it has reached 21 m
at the Fota Arboretum, County Cork.

First planted at Chevithorne Barton in
1989. We have four trees, the tallest about
10 m, hardy.

We have recently received acorns of
what is probably the first introduction of
Q. trojana subsp. *euboica* (Papaioannou)
K.I. Chr., which is found only on the island
of Evia, Greece, and has the leaves white-
tomentose beneath.

(*Q. ilex* × *Q. robur*)

This hybrid was described from a plant raised and distributed in the late 18th century by the nurseryman Spencer Turner. It makes a medium-sized, semi-evergreen tree of rounded habit, retaining many of its leaves through the winter. Downy shoots bear elliptic to oblanceolate leathery leaves, to 10 cm long, edged with few shallow rounded lobes. They are hairy on both sides when young, becoming glossy dark green above, paler and thinly hairy beneath. The long female inflorescences to 10 cm or more with numerous flowers, show the influence of *Q. robur*. Acorns ovoid to 2 cm long, mostly not forming but occasionally one or two ripen on a stalk to 5 cm long. 'Pseudoturneri' is the most commonly see cultivar, usually grown as *Q.* ×*turneri*. It has reached 16 m at Kew.

Two of the three specimens at Chevithorne Barton are 'Pseudoturneri'. They are evergreen and hardy, the tallest about 4 m. The other is 'Gnom', a dwarf shrub from Döring Nursery, Germany.

Quercus uxoris McVaugh

W Mexico

A large, late deciduous tree growing to 25 m tall or more, the young shoots covered with a yellow tomentum. Leaves leathery, elliptic to obovate, to 30 cm long and 10 cm wide, pointed at the tip with up to fourteen prominent, bristle-tipped teeth on each side, tapered at the base to a stalk up to 5 cm long. Hairy when young then dark, slightly glossy green above with yellowish hairs beneath at first, before becoming almost smooth on both sides and turning yellow in autumn before they fall. Acorns ovoid to 2 cm long, ripening the second year and borne singly or in clusters of up to three on a short stalk. It is listed as Vulnerable in the Red List of Oaks.

Introduced from Jalisco, Mexico, by Allen Coombes in 1995, but rare in cultivation.

We have tried to grow this oak out of doors at Chevithorne Barton three times but failed. We therefore keep one permanently in the greenhouse, where it has reached 2.5 m. It has very attractive large leaves.

Chinese cork oak
Japan, Korea, China, Taiwan

A large deciduous tree reaching 30 m tall, with a characteristic corky bark and downy young shoots. Leaves oblong to lanceolate, to 20 cm long and 5 cm wide, tapered to a point at the tip, rounded at the base with a stalk to 2 cm long. Up to sixteen pairs of parallel veins end in short, bristle-tipped teeth. They emerge densely covered in white hairs, becoming glossy dark green above with a persistent grey tomentum beneath. Acorns ovoid to nearly rounded, to 2.5 cm long, ripening the second year and borne singly in an unstalked cup densely covered in recurved scales. In several parts of China this species is grown for its cork, and the acorns are fed to pigs.

Introduced by Robert Fortune in 1861, it has reached 22 m at Windsor Great Park.

First planted at Chevithorne Barton in 1993, three trees here are growing rather slowly. They are between 4.5 and 5 m tall.

Quercus velutina Lam.

Black oak, Yellow-bark oak
E North America

A fast-growing, large deciduous tree often found on dry and sandy soils, growing to 25 or 30 m tall, with stout shoots that are smooth, or nearly so, when mature. Leaves elliptic in outline to 30 cm long and 15 cm across, rather shallowly to deeply cut into seven–nine lobes that are further divided, ending in numerous bristle-tipped teeth. They emerge densely covered in velvety red hairs when young, becoming glossy dark green above, green and sparsely hairy or nearly smooth beneath, and turning yellow-brown to red-brown in autumn. Acorns ovoid to nearly rounded, to 2 cm long, ripening the second year.

Introduced in 1800, it has reached 28 m at Colesbourne Park, Gloucestershire.

This tree grows satisfactorily, if rather slowly, at Chevithorne Barton. There are various cultivars in our collection, including 'Habiflax' which has big dark shiny leaves, and 'Oakridge Walker', a form with deeply cut leaves found in Illinois by Guy Sternberg. 'Rubrifolia', planted in a shaded position, is 8.5 m.

left: *Q. velutina* 'Oakridge Walker'
centre, right: *Q. velutina*

Quercus virginiana Mill

Live oak
SE United States

A magnificent, large evergreen tree found in low-lying areas of the coastal plain, where it is frequently seen draped with Spanish moss. It can reach 30 m tall but is often lower, and wide-spreading when growing in the open. Leaves very variable in shape, ovate to oblong or obovate, to about 10 cm long and 5 cm across, sometime larger, untoothed or with a few teeth on each side, especially on vigorous shoots. They are glossy dark green above and whitish or bluish-white beneath. Acorns ovoid to 2 or 2.5 cm long with a rounded tip, ripening the first year and borne singly or in clusters of up to three on a short stalk.

Introduced in 1739. We have two small specimens at Chevithorne Barton. They are growing, but very slowly, the larger being just over 2 m tall.

This tree is so venerated where it grows that the Live Oak Society is dedicated to its promotion. Only one of its members is human (the chairman): all the others are live oaks!

Q. fusiformis Small. The Texas live oak is an inland relative of *Q. virginiana*, found in Texas, Oklahoma and northeastern Mexico. It generally makes a smaller tree, sometimes shrubby, and differs in its pointed acorns. In its typical form it is a distinct tree but intermediates occur. Several introductions have been made in recent years from both the United States and Mexico. We have a small plant in our nursery.

right: *Q. virginiana*

Turkey

A large, spreading, deciduous tree to 25 m or more in height, found in mountain forests at about 1,500 m and above, where it grows with *Cedrus libani*. Leaves on a stalk to 3.5 cm long, obovate to 17 cm long and 10 cm across, deeply cut, sometimes almost to the midrib into up to seven lobes on each side, each one often with smaller secondary lobes. They are dark green above, paler and thinly hairy beneath, turning yellow in autumn. Acorns cylindrical to ovoid, to 3.5 cm long, ripening the first year and sessile or on a very short stalk. It is listed as Near Threatened in the Red List of Oaks.

Introduced in 1990 by Mark Flanagan and Mark Pitman, then both of Kew Gardens, it had reached 8 m at Kew.

We have one at Chevithorne Barton, in the Rifle Range, about 2.5 m tall.

Quercus wislizeni A. DC.

Interior live oak
California

An evergreen tree, sometimes shrubby, reaching 20 m tall and found in valleys and on mountain slopes. Leaves ovate to lanceolate, to 7 cm long and 5 cm across, tapered at the tip to a sharp point and edged with up to eight teeth on each side, or entire. Often opening bronze, they become glossy dark green above, paler and smooth beneath. Acorns narrow conical, gradually tapering to a pointed tip, to 4 cm long, ripening the second year, sessile or on a very short stalk.

Introduced in 1874, it has reached 17 m at Hillier Gardens.

The two trees here at Chevithorne Barton are 5.5 and 7 m high, fast-growing and tough but a bit susceptible to wind damage.

Q. ×kewensis Osborn (*Q. cerris × Q. wislizeni*). This hybrid was raised at Kew in 1914 from seed of *Q. wislizeni*. It makes a spreading evergreen, or semi-evergreen, tree to 10 m or more. The ovate leaves to 8 cm long are pointed at the tip, and shallowly and irregularly cut into pointed lobes. Acorns to 2.5 cm long but often not maturing. It has reached 9 m at Kew. This is probably the only known hybrid between a red oak (section *Lobatae*) and a white oak (section *Cerris*). We have a good specimen of this hybrid, planted in the Tapir Orchard in 1989, also at 9 m tall.

Q. parvula Greene. The Coast oak is restricted to Santa Cruz Island and a small area on the adjacent mainland in California. It is closely related to *Q. wislizeni* but normally makes a large shrub with rather dull green leaves and stalked acorns that only taper near the tip. It is listed as Endangered in the Red List of Oaks. We have two good specimens of this oak, both 4 m high. They are growing fast and are hardy.

top left, bottom left: *Q. wislizeni*
right: *Q. ×kewensis*

As well as growing oaks at Chevithorne Barton we are also developing a collection of *Lithocarpus*. Currently we have twelve different species. Although in the same family as the oaks (Fagaceae) and bearing acorns, these trees are, in fact, more closely related to the chestnuts (*Castanea*). It is a large genus of some 300 species of evergreen trees, more rarely shrubs, native from the Himalaya to Japan, and found predominantly in China and Southeast Asia, with one species (probably a separate genus – see cladogram page 30) in western North America. They differ from oaks in their upright flower.

L. corneus (Lour.) Rehder

S China, Taiwan

An evergreen tree to 15 m tall. Leaves elliptic to oblanceolate, to 15 cm long and 5 cm across, entire below the middle and narrowed, toothed in the upper part, ending in a tapered point, green on both sides. Acorns large, rounded to top-shaped in a cup to 5 cm across, ripening the second year.

Introduced from Taiwan by Allen Coombes in 2003.

We have two specimens from this introduction. They have survived two winters and look good. The tallest is about 1 m.

L. edulis (Makino) Nakai

Japan

A small evergreen tree, often a large shrub, to 10 m tall with glabrous shoots. The untoothed leathery leaves, to 15 cm long and 5 cm wide, are pointed at the tip and tapered to the base. They are dark green above with a metallic sheen beneath. Acorns cylindrical, with a pointed tip to 2.5 cm long, borne in upright spikes to 8 cm long, and ripening the second year.

Introduced in the early 19th century, it has reached 16 m at Wakehurst Place, West Sussex.

This tree grows well here. There are four specimens in different areas. They start off as bushes and develop into trees with time and judicious pruning. The biggest has grown to about 5 m in ten years.

L. hancei (Benth.) Rehder

S China, Taiwan

A spreading, evergreen tree to 15 m tall, with glabrous shoots. Leaves untoothed, elliptic to lanceolate, to 10 cm long and 5 cm wide, tapered to a point at the tip and narrowed at the base to a stalk up to 4 cm long, green on both sides. Acorns nearly rounded with a short point at the tip to 2 cm long, ripening the second year. It has reached 9 m at Caerhays, Cornwall.

Our plants are from seed collected in Taiwan by Allen Coombes in 2003. We have two trees from this introduction. They are healthy and apparently fairly hardy. One, planted in the Rifle Range, is an experiment to see whether it will flourish in an exposed site.

L. kawakamii (Hayata) Hayata

Taiwan

An evergreen tree to 15 m tall or more. Leaves obovate or oblong, leathery, to 25 cm long and 7 cm wide. Abruptly narrowed at the tip to a point and toothed above the middle, tapering at the base to a stalk up to 5 cm long. Acorns rounded, 2.5 cm long, borne clustered on the shoots in a sessile, shallow cup and ripening the second year.

We have two trees from plants introduced by Allen Coombes in 2003. An earlier introduction by Tom Hudson grows in his garden at Tregrehan, Cornwall. Our trees have been planted out for two years and, rather surprisingly, look exceptionally good after a hard winter. The tallest is about 1.5 m.

L. lepidocarpus (Hayata) Hayata

Taiwan

A large evergreen tree in the wild, with lanceolate leaves to 30 cm long and 10 cm across, dark green above and whitish beneath. They are untoothed and taper at the tip to a long point. Acorns rounded, 2 cm long, usually completely enclosed in the thick, scaly cup, which is concave at the end.

It was introduced by Allen Coombes in 2003.

We have two trees of this oak from the 2003 introduction and after two seasons planted out, are healthy and happy. Like most *Lithocarpus*, they are evergreen in our climate. The tallest is about 1.2 m.

L. truncatus (King ex Hook. f.) Rehder

SE Asia

An evergreen tree growing to 30 m tall, with untoothed lanceolate leaves to 25 cm long and 7 cm across. They are glossy dark green above, glaucous and scaly beneath and taper to a fine point at the tip. Acorns rounded to 3 cm long with a rounded top, most of the acorn enclosed in the cup.

Introduced from Yunnan by Allen Coombes in 1998.

We have one young tree growing in the area above the Tapir Orchard, about 1.5 m tall. This is where most of the *Lithocarpus* are planted as the spot combines shelter with quite a bit of sun, and this seems to suit the genus.

L. variolosus (Franch.) Chun

SW China, N Vietnam

An evergreen tree to 20 m tall, with ovate to lanceolate, untoothed, usually wavy-edged leaves, to about 20 cm long and 5 cm across, the tip taper-pointed and often slightly twisted. They are dark green above and blue-green beneath. Acorns nearly rounded, 2.5 cm across, half or more enclosed in the cup.

Introduced in 1991 by Charlie Howick, this species, from relatively high altitudes in the mountains, is proving hardy and has already flowered and fruited in cultivation.

We have one tree from the 1991 introduction, which Charlie Howick gave us. It is now 3 m tall, evergreen, apparently hardy and in some years has a good crop of acorns, which come in bunches. However, the squirrels get them first, although I do not believe the acorns are fertile.

Acorns come in a wide range of shapes and sizes. A few have been chosen here to demonstrate their diversity.

1.

Quercus michauxii
collected by Mike Frampton-Price in Maryland, USA.

2.

Quercus coccifera
collected by Octavian von Hofmannsthal in Greece.

3.

Quercus
hybrid at Chevithorne Barton.

4.

Lithocarpus pachyphyllus
is from East Asia but this seed was collected at Caerhays, Cornwall, where it grows successfully and produces fertile seed.

5.

Quercus stenophylloides
photographed by Allen Coombes in Taiwan.

6.

Lithocarpus elegans
from Bhutan, but found across East Asia.

(continues on following spread)

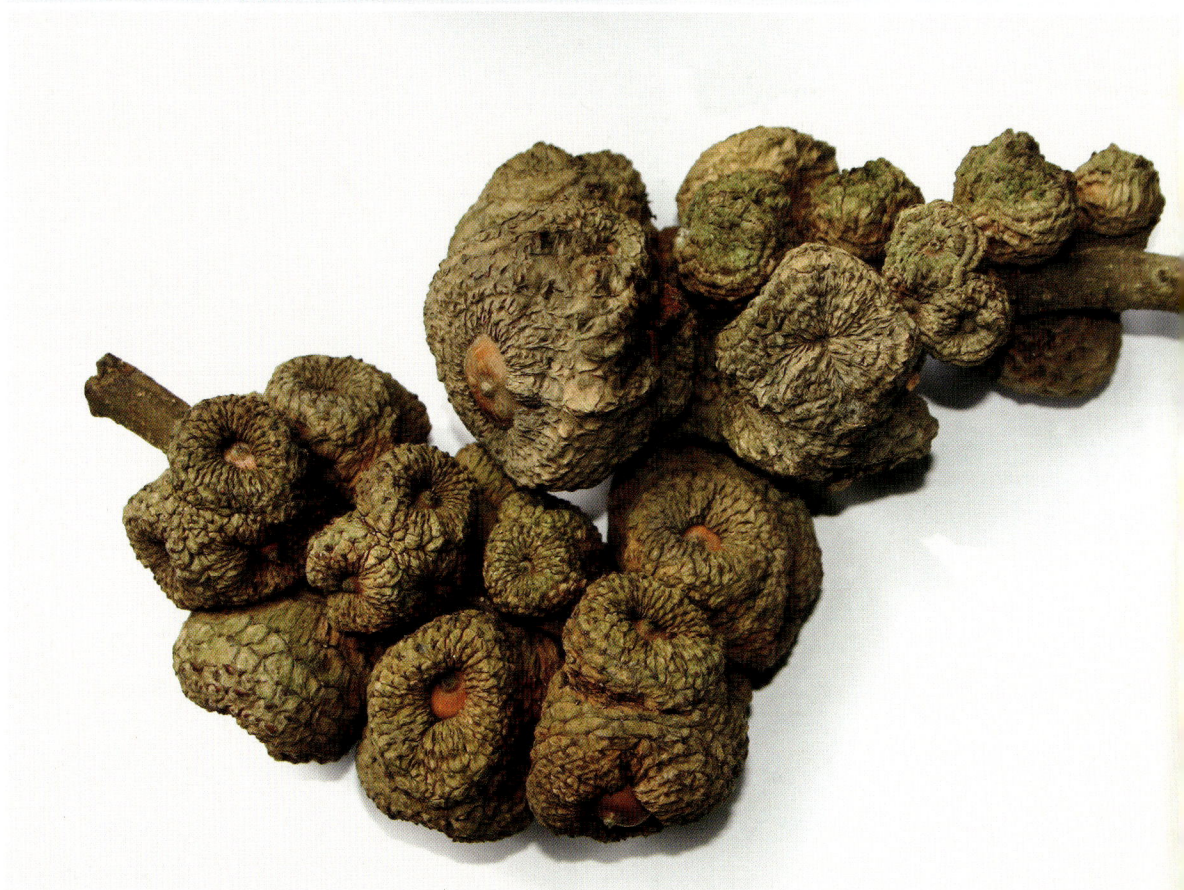

1	2	3
4	5	6

Quercus argyrotricha
photographed by Allen Coombes in China.

8.
Quercus robur
Pendula Group at Chevithorne Barton.

9.
Quercus glabrescens
at Chevithorne Barton, seed originally from
Mexico.

10.
Quercus cerris
acorn collected by Jane MacEwen from
Badminton, Gloucestershire, compared to a
Q. insignis acorn from Mexico, the largest of
all acorns: this one had a width of 52mm.

11.
Quercus dolicholepis
photographed by Allen Coombes in China.

7	8	
9	10	11

Oaks are found across many regions in the northern hemisphere. The following pages demonstrate just a few areas where oaks, which are represented in the National Collection® at Chevithorne Barton, are found. Collecting from higher altitudes increases the chances of the species being able to be grown in Devon.

1.
Mexico
Mixed oak and pine forest in the Chapinque Ecological Park, near Monterrey, the habitat of *Quercus rysophylla*. Mexico has the greatest number of species of oaks to be found, with new species continually being described.

2. & 3.
Taiwan
Collecting *Quercus salicina* from a rocky ridge in northern Taiwan.

4.
China
View of the Mangshan in souhern Yunnan. Plants of *Q. obovatifolia* can be seen in the foreground.

Photographs by Allen Coombes

Bhutan has a diverse range of habitats: one of the oak species, *Quercus griffithii*, is particularly important, providing firewood, leaf litter for agriculture and wood for building.

1.
Ugyencholing Palace in the Tang Valley, Bumthang, central Bhutan. The tree on the left of the picture is *Quercus griffithii*.

2.
Mountain ranges near the top of Thurumsingh La Pass, central Bhutan. In this habitat are found such species as *Quercus lanata*, *Q. lamellosa* and *Lithocarpus pachyphyllus*.

3. & 4.
Q. griffithii in eastern Bhutan, near Jyonkhar.

Photographs by Belinda Edwards

Views of the snow peaks of the Kawa Kharpo range across the river gorge from stupas, on the east bank of the Upper Mekong.

1.
Scrub oaks (probably *Q. aquifolioides*) can be seen growing in the foreground of the six stupas shown. (Altitude 3,550 m)

2.
The holy mountain range of Kawa Karpo (Meili Xueshan in Chinese). Circum-navigation of the whole massif represents a Buddhist pilgrimage of roughly 300 km, which pilgrims complete in two to three weeks, along sometimes dangerous footpaths. On the right-hand side of the photograph is a scrub oak with prayer flags attached to it.

3.
Oak with (possibly) turnips being dried in the background. Photographed in October near Pomda, eastern Tibetan Autonomous Region. (Altitude *c.* 4,000 m).

4.
Stupas photographed at dawn on Mount Baima, on the eastern side of the Upper Mekong gorge. The hills shown have scrub oaks growing on them.

Photographs by Carol Turner

1		
3	4	2

Map of Chevithorne Barton

Legend

AO	Apple Orchard
DR	Drive
ESD	East of Sheep Dip
FBH	Field below House
GH	Greenhouse Bench (GHB) & Cold Frame (GHCF)
H	House
KG	Kitchen Garden
NOTO	North of Tapir Orchard
OTCF	Old Tennis Court Field
PT	Polytunnel
R	Rookery
ROCK	Rockery (beside greenhouse)
RRET	Rifle Range East Triangle
RRN	Rifle Range North
RRNE	Rifle Range North East
RRP	Rifle Range Pentagon
RRSE	Rifle Range South East
RRSET	Rifle Range South East Triangle
RRST	Rifle Range South Triangle
RRSWT	Rifle Range South West Triangle
SDH	Sheep Dip Hedge
SP	Swimming Pool
TC	Tennis Court
TOE	Tapir Orchard East
TOW	Tapir Orchard West
WG	Walled Garden
WOC	Walnut Orchard Central
WOE	Walnut Orchard East
WOW	Walnut Orchard West
WOTO	West of Tapir Orchard
WGNOS	Woodland Garden North of Stream
WGSOS	Woodland Garden South of Stream

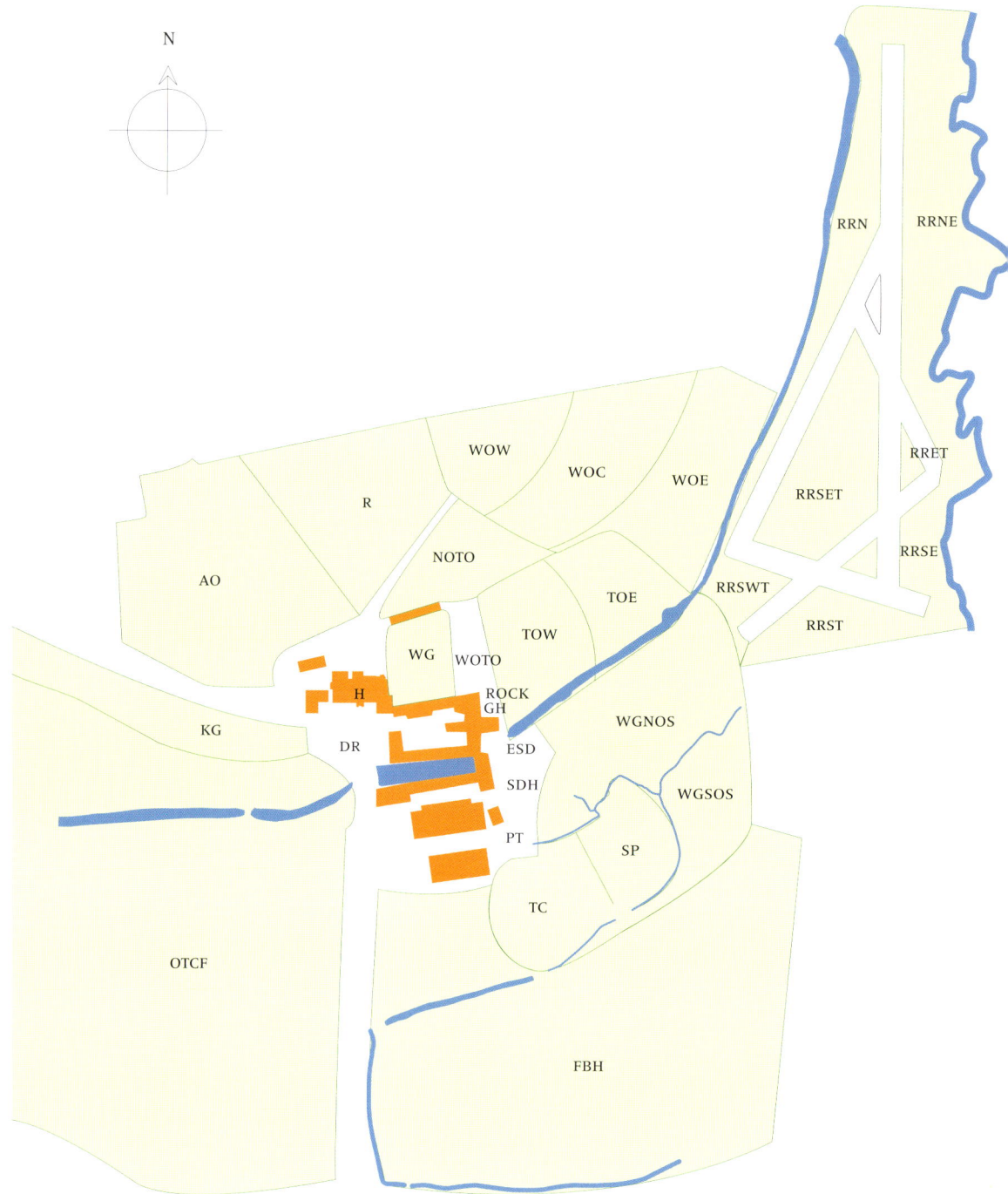

N

Analogous
  Of similar structure and function but with a different origin.

Appressed
  Flattened against a surface.

Axil
  The angle formed where two structures, such as veins, meet.

Cultivar
  A form selected and propagated for a particular, usually ornamental, quality.

Cupule
  The distinctive cup holding an acorn.

Deciduous
  A plant that loses all or most of its leaves at a particular time of year, usually autumn.

Elliptic
  Broadest in the centre, narrowing to each end.

Elliptic-oblong
  Between elliptic and oblong.

Epithet, specific
  A word which, when it follows the name of a genus, forms the complete name of a species. For example in the name *Quercus insignis*, the name of the genus is *Quercus*, the specific epithet is *insignis*.

Glabrous
  Without hairs.

Glaucous
  Bluish white.

Homologous
  Of similar structure and origin.

Impressed
  Sunken.

Inrolled
  Curved inwards.

Knopper gall
  An abnormal growth on an acorn formed as a response to the wasp *Andricus quercuscalicis*, which lays its eggs on the young acorns of *Quercus robur*.

Lanceolate
  Broadest towards the base, narrowed to the tip and more than three times as long as wide.

Leat
  A man-made stream leading to a mill.

Lobed / unlobed
  With or without relatively deep indentations.

Monophyletic
  A group of organisms consisting of an ancestor and all its descendants.

Oblanceolate
  Broadest towards the end, narrowed to the base and more than three times as long as wide.

Oblong
  Longer than broad with more or less parallel sides.

Obovate
  Broadest towards the end, narrowed to the base and less than three times as long as wide.

Ovate
  Broadest towards the base, narrowed to the tip and less than three times as long as wide.

Ovoid
  Egg-shaped, broadest at the base.

Pachydermatous
  Resembling the hide of an elephant.

Petiole
  The stalk of a leaf.

Recurved
  Curved backwards.

Reticulate
  With a distinctly visible network of veins.

Scales
  Small, flattened structures such as found on a leaf or acorn cup.

Sessile
  Without a stalk.

Sinus
  The indentation between the lobes of a leaf.

Taper-pointed
  Gradually narrowing to a point.

Tomentose
  Covered with a layer of dense matted hairs.

Tomentum
  A covering of dense matted hairs.

Approximate metric imperial conversion table

1 cm = 0.4 in	1 in = 2.54 cm
5 cm = 2 in	1 ft = 30.48 cm
10 cm = 4 in	
20 cm = 8 in	
1 m = 3 ft 3 in	
2 m = 6 ft 6 in	
5m = 16 ft 5 in	
7 m = 23 ft	
10 m = 33 ft 3 in	
30 m = 100 ft	

Appendices

Fast-growing oaks

A selection of oaks that grow faster than average and are hardy at Chevithorne Barton.

* These grow exceptionally fast, up to 1.5 m a year.

Q. acherdophylla *
Q. acutifolia
Q. acutissima
Q. affinis *
Q. agrifolia
Q. canariensis
Q. candicans
Q. castaneifolia 'Green Spire' *
Q. chrysolepis
Q. coccinea 'Splendens'
Q. conspersa
Q. crassifolia
Q. durifolia
Q. ellipsoidalis
Q. engelmannii
Q. falcata
Q. georgiana
Q. ×heterophylla
Q. ×hispanica cultivars
Q. imbricaria
Q. laurina
Q. ×libanerris *
Q. mexicana
Q. myrsinifolia
Q. oxyodon
Q. palustris
Q. pyrenaica 'Pendula'
Q. phillyreoides
Q. rysophylla
Q. sartorii
Q. ×turneri 'Pseudoturneri'
Q. wislizeni
Q. velutina 'Rubrifolia' *

Champion trees

The following specimens at Chevithorne Barton were measured by Dr Owen Johnson, Assistant Registrar of the Tree Register, in early May 2007, and appear on the TROBI (Tree Register of the British Isles) website as Champion Trees.

Q. acherdophylla in Woodland Garden South of Stream (WGSOS): 10 m high, stem 14 cm in diameter, girth 44 cm measured 1.5 m from the ground.

Q. affinis in Tennis Court (TC): 9 m high, stem 21 cm in diameter, girth 66 cm measured 1.5 m from the ground.

Q. candicans in area West of Tapir Orchard (WOTO): 9 m high, stem 17 cm in diameter, girth 53 cm measured 1.5 m from the ground

Q. ×hispanica 'Waasland Select' in Tapir Orchard East (TOE): 6 m high, stem 27 cm in diameter, girth 85 cm measured 1m from the ground.

Q. ×hispanica 'Wageningen' in Tapir Orchard West (TOW): 9 m high, stem 24 cm in diameter, girth 75 cm measured 1m from the ground.

Q. ×libanerris in Woodland Garden North of Stream (WGNOS): 11 m high, stem 21 cm in diameter, girth 66 cm measured 1.5 m from the ground.

Other large specimens noted in Owen Johnson's report include:

Q. acutifolia in Rifle Range Pentage (RRP): 4 m high, stem 11 cm in diameter measured at 1.2 m from the ground.

Q. crassipes in Walnut Orchard Central (WOC): 10 m high, stem 10 cm in diameter measured 1.3 m from the ground.

Q. ×libanerris 'Trompenburg' in Tapir Orchard West (TOW): 9 m high, stem 20 cm in diameter measured 1.5 m from the ground.

Q. rubra 'Cyrille' in Walnut Orchard East (WOE): 10.5 m high, stem 14 cm in diameter measured 1.5 cm from the ground.

Q. schottkyana in Woodland Garden North of Stream (WGNOS): 9 m high, stem 10 cm in diameter measured 1.5 m from the ground.

Notable American white oaks

American white oaks at Chevithorne Barton that have grown to at least 3 m.

Q. bicolor
Q. douglasii
Q. engelmannii
Q. lobata
Q. lyrata
Q. macrocarpa
Q. montana
Q. muehlenbergii

Winter-tolerant White Mexican oaks

Mexican oaks at Chevithorne Barton, cut back by winter frost 2005-06, (the worst winter of the decade), but which survived.

Q. castanea × *Q. eduardii*
Q. castanea × *Q. sapotifolia*
Q. germana
Q. insignis
Q. lancifolia
Q. leiophylla
Q. peduncularis
Q. planipocula
Q. rugosa
Q. sapotifolia
Q. sartorii
Q. subspathulata

Threatened oaks

The existence of the following species in the collection at Chevithorne Barton are threatened in their wild locations. Data from the IUCN Red List of Oaks, published by Fauna and Flora International in 2007.

Q. acerifolia (Endangered)
Q. alnifolia (Vulnerable)
Q. argyrotricha (Endangered)
Q. arkansana (Vulnerable)
Q. aucheri (Near Threatened)
Q. dumosa (Endangered)
Q. faginea subsp. *alpestris* (Endangered)
Q. georgiana (Endangered)
Q. germana (Vulnerable)
Q. insignis (Near Threatened)
Q. miquihuanensis (Endangered)
Q. oglethorpensis (Endangered)
Q. pacifica (Vulnerable)
Q. parvula (Endangered)
Q. polymorpha (Near Threatened)
Q. pontica (Vulnerable)
Q. rotundifolia (Near Threatened)
Q. rysophylla (Near Threatened)
Q. subspathulata (Vulnerable)
Q. tomentella (Vulnerable)
Q. uxoris (Vulnerable)
Q. vulcanica (Near Threatened)

List of the collection

This is a complete list of the collection as of February 2009. The map location codes relate to the legend of the map found on page 203. The group names indicate at a glance if the species belongs to subgenus *Cyclobalanopsis*, subgenus *Quercus* section *Quercus* (the white oaks), subgenus *Quercus* section *Lobatae* (the red oaks), subgenus *Quercus* section *Protobalanus* (the intermediate oaks), or to the provisional subgenus *Quercus* section *Cerris* – see page 32 for an account of the differences. Names in bold indicate specimens described in the main text – refer to the index (page 216) to find out on which page.

NAME	GROUP	COMMON NAME	PARENTAGE	NATURAL RANGE	MAP LOCATIONS
QUERCUS					
Q. acerifolia	Lobatae	Maple-leaf oak		Arkansas	WOE
Q. acherdophylla	Lobatae			Mexico	ESD - NOTO - WGSOS - WOC
Q. acuta	Cyclobalanopsis			Japan-S Korea-Taiwan	WGNOS - WGSOS
Q. ×acutidens	Quercus		Q. cornelius-mulleri × Q. engelmannii	SW California	GHB
Q. acutifolia	Lobatae			C & S Mexico-C America	GHB - NOTO - RRP - RRSET
Q. acutissima	Cerris	Sawtooth oak		China-Japan-Himalaya	TC - WGNOS
Q. affinis	Lobatae			Mexico	NOTO - SDH - TC - WGSOS - WOE
Q. agrifolia	Lobatae	Coast live oak		California-North Mexico	ESD - GHB - SDH - SP - WOC
Q. agrifolia var. oxyadenia	Lobatae			Baja California-S California	GHB
Q. alba	Quercus	White oak		E North America	R
Q. alba 'Elongata'	Quercus				RRN
Q. alba 'Gatton Grave'	Quercus				WOE
Q. alba 'Lincoln'	Quercus				RRP
Q. aliena	Quercus	Oriental white oak		Japan-Korea-China	WOE
Q. aliena var. acutiserrata	Quercus			Japan-China-Thailand	RRP
Q. aliena var. pekingensis	Quercus			N China	R - RRP
Q. alnifolia	Cerris	Golden oak of Cyprus		Cyprus	GHCF - ROCK - WOTO
Q. ×alvordiana	Quercus		Q. douglasii × Q. john-tuckeri	CW California	RRP
Q. ×andegavensis	Quercus		Q. pyrenaica × Q. robur	SW Europe	RRS
Q. ×andegavensis 'Staatspark Karlsaue'	Quercus		Q. pyrenaica × Q. robur		RRSE
Q. aquifolioides	Quercus			W China	GHB
Q. argyrotricha	Cyclobalanopsis			China	GHCF - NOTO
Q. arizonica	Quercus	Arizona white oak		SW United States-North Mexico	GHCF - RRSE
Q. arkansana	Lobatae	Arkansas oak		Florida-Texas	ESD - WOC
Q. ×atlantica	Lobatae		Q. incana × Q. laurifolia	SE United States	RRS
Q. aucheri	Cerris			Aegean Is.-SW Turkey	ROCK
Q. ×audleyensis	Cerris × Quercus		Q. ilex × Q. petraea		WGNOS
Q. austrina	Quercus	Bluff oak		SE United States	RRNE - WOC
Q. baloot	Cerris			Himalaya	ROCK
Q. baronii	Quercus			W China	GHCF
Q. "bastardica"	Quercus		Q. turbinella? × Q. virginiana?		FBH
Q. ×bebbiana	Quercus		Q. alba × Q. macrocarpa	E United States	ESD
Q. ×bebbiana 'Taco'	Quercus		Q. alba × Q. macrocarpa		FBH

NAME	GROUP	COMMON NAME	PARENTAGE	NATURAL RANGE	MAP LOCATIONS
Q. berberidifolia	Quercus	California scrub oak		SW California-North Mexico	GHB - ROCK
Q. bicolor	Quercus	Swamp white oak		E North America-SE Canada	NOTO
Q. 'Bill George'	Quercus		*Q. robur × Q. sadleriana*		RRP
Q. brantii	Cerris			SW Asia	RRNE - WOC
Q. ×brittonii	Lobatae		*Q. ilicifolia × Q. marilandica*	NE United States	GHCF
Q. buckleyi	Lobatae	Buckley oak		Oklahoma-Texas	NOTO
Q. ×bushii	Lobatae		*Q. marilandica × Q. velutina*	E United States	GHCF - RRN - RRP - WGNOS
Q. canariensis	Quercus	Algerian oak		N Africa-SW Europe	GHCF - RRNE - RRST - TOW
Q. canbyi	Lobatae			Mexico	ESD - GHB
Q. candicans	Lobatae			Mexico-Guatemala	GHB - RRNE - WOC - WOTO
Q. ×capesii	Lobatae		*Q. nigra × Q. phellos*	E United States	WOC
Q. castanea	Lobatae			Mexico Guatemala	GHB - NOTO - SDH
Q. castanea × Q. eduardii	Lobatae			Mexico	RRNE
Q. castanea × Q. sapotifolia	Lobatae			Mexico	RRP - RRSET
Q. castaneifolia	Cerris	Chestnut-leaved oak		S & C Europe-N Iran	FBH - NOTO - WOC - WOE
Q. castaneifolia **'Green Spire'**	Cerris				RRST - WGNOS
Q. castaneifolia 'Sopron'	Cerris				WOC
Q. cedrosensis	Protobalanus			North Mexico	GHB
Q. cerris	Cerris	Turkey oak		S & C Europe-Turkey	FBH - WOC - WOW
Q. cerris **'Argenteovariegata'**	Cerris				WGNOS
Q. cerris 'Donar'	Cerris				TOE
Q. cerris 'Marmor Star'	Cerris				RRNE
Q. cerris **'Wodan'**	Cerris				AO
Q. championii	Cyclobalanopsis			SE China-Hainan-Taiwan	GHB
Q. chapmanii	Quercus	Chapman oak		SE United States	NOTO
Q. chenii	Cerris			SE China	TC - WGNOS - WGSOS - WOE
Q. chrysolepis	Protobalanus	Canyon live oak		SW United States-NW Mexico	GHB - WGNOS
Q. chrysolepis × Q. tomentella	Protobalanus			Channel Is., California	RRP
Q. coccifera	Cerris	Kermes oak		Mediterranean region	GHCF - WGNOS
Q. coccifera subsp. *calliprinos*	Cerris	Palestine oak		E Mediterranean region	WGNOS - WGSOS
Q. coccifera subsp. *rivasmartinezii*	Cerris			Portugal	ROCK
Q. coccinea	Lobatae	Scarlet oak		E North America	AO - RRP
Q. coccinea 'Splendens'	Lobatae				RRSET - TOW
Q. coccolobifolia	Quercus			Mexico	GHB

NAME	GROUP	COMMON NAME	PARENTAGE	NATURAL RANGE	MAP LOCATIONS
Q. ×comptoniae	Quercus	Compton oak	Q. lyrata × Q. virginiana	S United States	R
Q. conspersa	Lobatae			S Mexico-C America	NOTO - WOC
Q. cornelius-mulleri	Quercus	Muller oak		S California-North Mexico	GHB
Q. costaricensis	Lobatae			Costa Rica	GHB
Q. crassifolia	Lobatae			Mexico-C America	GHB - RRP - WGSOS
Q. crassipes	Lobatae			Mexico	GHB - RRP - WOC
Q. crispipilis	Lobatae			S Mexico-Guatemala	WGSOS
Q. cubana	Quercus			Cuba	GHC
Q. cupreata	Lobatae			NE Mexico	GHB
Q. dalechampii	Quercus			E Europe	NOTO - RRP
Q. ×deamii	Quercus		Q. macrocarpa × Q. muehlenbergii	C United States	FBH - GHCF
Q. dentata	Quercus	Daimio oak		Japan-NE Asia	ESD - RRP - SP
Q. dentata 'Carl Ferris Miller'	Quercus				WOE
Q. dentata × Q. griffithii	Quercus			Yunnan	RRP
Q. dentata × Q. malacotricha	Quercus			Yunnan	RRNE
Q. dentata 'Pinnatifida'	Quercus				WGNOS
Q. dentata × Q. yunnanensis	Quercus			Yunnan	WOW
Q. deserticola	Quercus			Mexico	RRP
Q. dolicholepis	Cerris			C & SW China	RRP - WGSOS
Q. 'Döring's Zweizack'	Quercus				RRNE
Q. douglasii	Quercus	Blue oak		California	GHCF - WGSOS
Q. dumosa	Quercus	Nuttall scrub oak		S California-North Mexico	GHB - WOTO
Q. durata	Quercus	Leather oak		California	ROCK
Q. durifolia	Lobatae			Mexico	ESD
Q. ×dysophylla	Lobatae		Q. crassifolia × Q. crassipes	Mexico	GHB - RRP
Q. eduardii	Lobatae			Mexico	GHB
Q. ellipsoidalis	Lobatae	Northern pin oak		C United States-S Ontario	WGSOS
Q. ellipsoidalis 'Hemelrijk'	Lobatae				WOE
Q. emoryi	Lobatae	Emory oak		SW United States-Mexico	RRP - WOC
Q. emoryi × Q. hypoleucoides	Lobatae				WGNOS
Q. engelmannii	Quercus	Engelmann oak		S California-North Mexico	GHB - WOTO
Q. aff. eugeniifolia	Lobatae			Mexico-C America	GHB - WGNOS
Q. ×exacta	Lobatae		Q. imbricaria × Q. palustris	N United States	FBH
Q. fabri	Quercus			E & SE China	GHCF - WGNOS - WOC
Q. faginea	Quercus	Portuguese oak		Spain-Portugal-N Africa	GHCF - WGNOS - WGSOS
Q. faginea subsp. alpestris	Quercus			S Spain	RRSE
Q. faginea subsp. broteroi	Quercus			S Spain-S Portugal-N Africa	TC - WOC
Q. faginea × Q. canariensis	Quercus			Spain-Morocco	RRST
Q. falcata	Lobatae	Southern red oak		SE United States	FBH - KG
Q. ×fernaldii	Lobatae		Q. ilicifolia × Q. rubra	E United States	RRNE
Q. ×filialis	Lobatae		Q. phellos × Q. velutina	E United States	RRP
Q. fleuryi	Cyclobalanopsis			China-Vietnam	GHB
Q. frainetto	Quercus	Hungarian oak		Italy-SE Europe	WOE

NAME	GROUP	COMMON NAME	PARENTAGE	NATURAL RANGE	MAP LOCATIONS
Q. franchetii	Cerris			SW China-N Thailand	GHB - NOTO - RRNE
Q. fusiformis	Quercus	Texas live oak		SW United States-NE Mexico	GHB - GHCF
Q. galeanensis	Lobatae			NE Mexico	GHCF
Q. gambelii 'Los Lunas'	Quercus				R
Q. gambelii × *Q. macrocarpa*	Quercus				GHCF
Q. gambelii × *Q. sinuata*	Quercus				GHCF
Q. gambelii 'Yankee Red Head'	Quercus				R
Q. garryana	Quercus	Garry oak		W North America-California-Oregon	RRP - WOC
Q. garryana subsp. *breweri*	Quercus				GHCF
Q. geminata	Quercus	Sand live oak		SE United States	RRP
Q. georgiana	Lobatae	Georgia oak		Alabama-Georgia	WGSOS - WOE
Q. georgiana × *Q. nigra*	Lobatae			SE United States	RRST
Q. germana	Quercus			Mexico	GHB - RRSWT - WGSOS
Q. gilva	Cyclobalanopsis			China-Taiwan-Japan	NOTO - WOC
Q. glabrescens	Quercus			Mexico	GHCF - SDH
Q. glauca	Cyclobalanopsis	Japanese blue oak		E Asia	GHCF
Q. glauca var. *amamiana*	Cyclobalanopsis			Japan	GHB
Q. glauca var. *gracilis*	Cyclobalanopsis			China	GHB
Q. graciliramis	Lobatae			Nuevo Leon, Mexico	GHB
Q. gravesii	Lobatae	Chisos red oak		SW Texas-North Mexico	GHCF - KG
Q. greggii	Quercus			Mexico	GHB - GHCF - ROCK
Q. griffithii	Quercus			Himalaya-SE Asia	GHCF - RRP
Q. grisea	Quercus	Grey oak		SW United States-Mexico	GHCF - KG
Q. guajavifolia	Cerris			Sichuan Yunnan	WOTO
Q. hartwissiana	Quercus			E Bulgaria-Turkey	RRN - WOC
Q. ×hastingsii	Lobatae		*Q. buckleyi* × *Q. marilandica*	Texas	RRP - WOC
Q. havardii	Quercus	Shin oak		SC United States	RRNE
Q. havardii × *Q. stellata*	Quercus			S United States	GHCF
Q. hemisphaerica	Lobatae	Darlington oak		SE United States	KG - WGSOS - WOE
Q. ×heterophylla	Lobatae		*Q. phellos* × *Q. rubra*	E United States	NOTO - RRP
Q. ×hickelii	Quercus		*Q. pontica* × *Q. robur*		WGSOS
Q. ×hickelii 'Giesselhorst'	Quercus		*Q. pontica* × *Q. robur*		WOE
Q. hinckleyi	Quercus	Hinckley oak		Texas-North Mexico	GHCF
Q. hintoniorum	Lobatae			Mexico	GHCF
Q. hirtifolia	Lobatae			Mexico	GHB
Q. ×hispanica 'Ambrozyana'	Cerris		*Q. cerris* × *Q. suber*		WGSOS
Q. ×hispanica 'Brünn'	Cerris		*Q. cerris* × *Q. suber*		RRN
Q. ×hispanica 'Diversifolia'	Cerris		*Q. cerris* × *Q. suber*		FBH
Q. ×hispanica 'Fulhamensis'	Cerris	Fulham oak	*Q. cerris* × *Q. suber*		RRNE
Q. ×hispanica 'Lucombeana'	Cerris	Lucombe oak	*Q. cerris* × *Q. suber*		D - OTCF
Q. ×hispanica 'Waasland Select'	Cerris		*Q. cerris* × *Q. suber*		KG - R - RRNE - TOE
Q. ×hispanica 'Wageningen'	Cerris		*Q. cerris* × *Q. suber*		TOW
Q. hondae	Cyclobalanopsis			Kyushu, Japan	GHB

NAME	GROUP	COMMON NAME	PARENTAGE	NATURAL RANGE	MAP LOCATIONS
Q. humboldtii	Lobatae			Colombia-Panama	GHB
Q. hypoleucoides	Lobatae	Silverleaf oak		SW United States-North Mexico	NOTO
Q. ilex	Cerris	Evergreen oak		Mediterranean region	NOTO - OTCF - RRP - RRSWT - WGNOS - WGSOS
Q. ilex **'Fordii'**	Cerris				FBH
Q. ilex 'Refugiorum'	Cerris				WGSOS
Q. ilicifolia	Lobatae	Bear oak		NE United States-S Ontario	GHCF - WGSOS
Q. ilicifolia × *Q. georgiana*	Lobatae				RRSWT
Q. ilicifolia **'Tromp Ball'**	Lobatae				WOE
Q. imbricaria	Lobatae	Shingle oak		SE & C United States	R - TOW - WOC - WOE
Q. incana	Lobatae	Bluejack oak		SE United States	TC - WOTO
Q. infectoria	Quercus			SE Europe-Turkey	SP
Q. infectoria subsp. ***veneris***	Quercus			Cyprus-SW Asia	NOTO
Q. insignis	Quercus			Mexico-C America	GHC
Q. intricata	Quercus	Coahuila scrub oak		Texas-North Mexico	ESD
Q. ×introgressa	Quercus		*Q. bicolor* × *Q. muehlenbergii* × *Q. prinoides*	Missouri	R
Q. invaginata	Quercus			N Mexico	GHB
Q. ithaburensis	Quercus			SW Asia	NOTO
Q. john-tuckeri	Quercus	Tucker oak		C & S California	GHB
Q. kelloggii	Lobatae	California black oak		California-Oregon	RRNE - WGNOS - WOTO
Q. ×kewensis	Cerris × Lobatae		*Q. cerris* × *Q. wislizeni*		TOW
Q. laceyi	Quercus	Lacey oak		Texas-North Mexico	GHB - NOTO
Q. laceyi × *Q. macrocarpa*	Quercus				GHCF
Q. laeta	Quercus			Mexico	WGNOS
Q. laevis	Lobatae	American turkey oak		SE United States	WGNOS
Q. lamellosa	Cyclobalanopsis			SW China-Himalaya	NOTO - WGNOS
Q. lanata	Quercus			Himalaya-SE Asia	GHB
Q. lancifolia	Lobatae			S Mexico-C America	NOTO - RRWT - WOE
Q. laurifolia	Lobatae	Laurel oak		SE United States	WGNOS
Q. laurina	Lobatae			Mexico	GHB - GHCF - NOTO - R
Q. ×leana	Lobatae		*Q. imbricaria* × *Q. velutina*	SE United States	WOC
Q. leucotrichophora	Cerris	Banj oak		Himalaya	GHCF - NOTO - RRP
Q. ×libanerris	Cerris		*Q. cerris* × *Q. libani*	Turkey	RRNE - WGNOS
Q. ×libanerris **'Rotterdam'**	Cerris		*Q. cerris* × *Q. libani*		RRET
Q. ×libanerris **'Trompenburg'**	Cerris		*Q. cerris* × *Q. libani*		RRET - TOW
Q. libani	Cerris	Lebanon oak		SW Asia	ESD - RRP
Q. liboensis	Cyclobalanopsis			Guizhou, China	GHCF
Q. liebmannii	Quercus			Mexico	GHCF
Q. lobata	Quercus	Valley oak		W California	RRNE - WGSOS
Q. lobata × *Q. macrocarpa*	Quercus				RRP
Q. longispica	Cerris			Yunnan-Sichuan	ROCK
Q. ×ludoviciana	Lobatae		*Q. pagoda* × *Q. phellos*	SE United States	GHCF
Q. lusitanica	Quercus			SW Europe-N Africa	NOTO - R - ROCK

NAME	GROUP	COMMON NAME	PARENTAGE	NATURAL RANGE	MAP LOCATIONS
Q. lyrata	Quercus	Overcup oak		SE United States	WGNOS - WOE
Q. ×macdanielii	Quercus		*Q. macrocarpa × Q. robur*		GHCF - RRN - RRP
Q. 'Macon'	Quercus		*Q. frainetto × Q. macranthera*		RRSE
Q. macranthera	Quercus			Caucasus-N Iran	RRSWT - WOE
Q. macranthera subsp. *syspirensis*	Quercus			C & N Turkey-Lebanon	NOTO - RRNE
Q. macrocarpa	Quercus	Bur oak		E North America	GHCF - RRN - TOW
Q. macrocarpa Les Barres form	Quercus				R
Q. macrocarpa × Q. pubescens	Quercus				GHCF
Q. macrolepis	Cerris	Valonia oak		SE Europe-Turkey	RRN - TC - WGNOS - WOE
Q. macrolepis 'Hemelrijk Silver'	Cerris				R - RRP
Q. ×mannifera	Quercus		*Q. infectoria* subsp. *veneris* × *Q. petraea* subsp. *Iberica*	SW Asia	WOC
Q. margaretta	Quercus	Sand post oak		SE United States	GHCF
Q. marilandica	Lobatae	Black Jack oak		E United States	RRP
Q. marilandica var. *ashei*	Lobatae			SC United States	GHCF
Q. 'Mauri'	Lobatae		*Q. rubra × Q. palustris*		RRN
Q. mexicana	Lobatae			Mexico	NOTO - RRNE - WOC
Q. michauxii	Quercus	Basket oak		SE United States	RRP - WGNOS
Q. microphylla	Quercus			Mexico	GHB
Q. miquihuanensis	Lobatae			Nuevo Leon-Tamaulipas, Mexico	WGNOS
Q. aff. *miquihuanensis*	Lobatae			Oaxaca, Mexico	GHB
Q. mohriana	Quercus	Mohr oak		W Texas-North Mexico	GHCF
Q. mongolica subsp. *crispula*	Quercus			E Russia-Japan	NOTO - RRP - TC
Q. monimotricha	Cerris			SW China-N Myanmar	WGNOS
Q. montana	Quercus	Chestnut oak		E United States	R - RRST - WOE
Q. ×morehus	Lobatae		*Q. kelloggii × Q. wislizeni*	California	GHCF - RRP
Q. morii	Cyclobalanopsis			Taiwan	GHCF - NOTO
Q. muehlenbergii	Quercus	Chinquapin oak		N America-North Mexico	GHCF
Q. multinervis	Cyclobalanopsis			China	GHB - GHCF - ROCK
Q. myrsinifolia	Cyclobalanopsis			S China-Laos-Japan	RRSET - TC - WGNOS
Q. nigra	Lobatae	Water oak		SE United States	TC - WGNOS - WOC - WOTO
Q. nigra 'Waasland'	Lobatae				WOC
Q. oblongifolia	Quercus	Mexican blue oak		SW United States-Mexico	WGNOS
Q. obtusata × Q. rugosa	Quercus			Mexico	RRET - RRP
Q. oglethorpensis	Quercus	Oglethorpe oak		Georgia, USA- S Carolina	GHCF - R
Q. oocarpa	Quercus			Costa Rica-Guatemala-Mexico-Panama	GHB
Q. oxyodon	Cyclobalanopsis			China-Himalaya	GHB - WOC
Q. pacifica	Quercus	Channel Islands scrub oak		Channel Is., California	GHB - ROCK - WGNOS
Q. pagoda	Lobatae	Cherrybark oak		E & SC United States	RRST - TC - WGSOS - WOE - WOW
Q. palmeri	Protobalanus	Palmer oak		California-Arizona-North Mexico	GHB

NAME	GROUP	COMMON NAME	PARENTAGE	NATURAL RANGE	MAP LOCATIONS
Q. palustris	Lobatae	Pin oak		E United States	WOE - WOTO
Q. palustris **'Compacta'**	Lobatae				OTCF - R - WOC
Q. palustris 'Karlsaue'	Lobatae				FBH
Q. palustris 'Pendula'	Lobatae				TC
Q. palustris **'Silhouette'**	Lobatae				OTCF - WOC
Q. palustris 'Umbraculifera'	Lobatae				TC
Q. palustris 'Windischleuba'	Lobatae				KG
Q. pannosa	Cerris			Yunnan-Sichuan	WGNOS
Q. parvula	Lobatae	Santa Cruz Island oak		C & S California-Channel Is., California	GHCF - RRP
Q. peduncularis	Quercus			Mexico-Guatemala	ESD
Q. pentacycla	Cyclobalanopsis			Yunnan	RRP - WGNOS
Q. petraea	Quercus	Durmast oak		Europe-Caucasus	AO - FBH - R
Q. petraea 'Acutiloba'	Quercus				WOE
Q. petraea 'Afghanistanensis'	Quercus				R
Q. petraea 'Cochleata'	Quercus				GHCF
Q. petraea subsp. *iberica*	Quercus			SW Asia	GHCF
Q. petraea 'Insecata'	Quercus				GHCF
Q. petraea **'Laciniata Crispa'**	Quercus				TOW
Q. petraea 'Muscaviensis'	Quercus				KG
Q. petraea subsp. *pinnatiloba*	Quercus			Turkey-Syria	GHCF
Q. petraea **'Purpurea'**	Quercus				WGNOS
Q. phellos	Lobatae	Willow oak		E United States	NOTO - WOE
Q. phellos **'Latifolia'**	Lobatae				R
Q. phillyreoides	Cerris	Ubame oak		China-Japan-Korea	SDH - TC - WG
Q. pinnativenulosa	Lobatae			E Mexico	GHB
Q. planipocula	Lobatae			Mexico	RRSET - WOC
Q. polycarpa	Quercus			Romania	WOC
Q. polymorpha	Quercus	Netleaf white oak		Texas-Mexico-Guatemala	GHB - WGSOS - WOTO
Q. **Pondaim Group**	Quercus		*Q. dentata* × *Q. pontica*		TC
Q. pontica	Quercus	Armenian oak		Caucasus-Turkey	NOTO - RRP - WGNOS
Q. potosina	Quercus			Mexico	GHCF
Q. prinoides	Quercus	Chinquapin oak		C & E United States-S Ontario	RRST
Q. "Procera"	Quercus				GHCF
Q. pseudosemecarpifolia	Cerris			SW China-Tibet	WGNOS - WGSOS
Q. pubescens	Quercus			Europe-Caucasus	KG - RRP - RRSE - TC - WGNOS
Q. pubescens subsp. *crispata*	Quercus			Turkey	WGNOS
Q. pubescens 'Dissecta'	Quercus				WOC
Q. pumila	Lobatae	Running oak		SE United States	NOTO
Q. pungens	Quercus	Sandpaper oak		SW United States-North Mexico	GHCF
Q. pyrenaica **'Pendula'**	Quercus				TC
Q. repanda	Quercus			Mexico	GHB

NAME	GROUP	COMMON NAME	PARENTAGE	NATURAL RANGE	MAP LOCATIONS
Q. ×richteri	Lobatae		*Q. palustris × Q. rubra*	E United States	WGSOS
Q. ×riparia	Lobatae		*Q. rubra × Q. shumardii*	Missouri	WOE
Q. robur	Quercus	Common oak		Europe-Caucasus	NOTO - R - RRSWT - WOE
Q. robur 'Argenteomarginata'	Quercus				TOW - WGNOS
Q. robur 'Castle Howard'	Quercus				R
Q. robur Cristata Group	Quercus				TOW - WOE
Q. robur 'Cupressoides'	Quercus				WGNOS
Q. robur subsp. *estremadurensis*	Quercus			Spain	KG
Q. robur 'Filicifolia'	Quercus				WOTO
Q. robur 'Fontäne'	Quercus				RRP
Q. robur 'Fürst Schwarzenburg'	Quercus				RRST
Q. robur 'Granbyana'	Quercus				R
Q. robur 'Heltorf'	Quercus				RRNE
Q. robur Heterophylla Group	Quercus				WOC
Q. robur 'Heterophylla Hentzei'	Quercus				RRP
Q. robur 'Hungaria'	Quercus				TOW
Q. robur subsp. *imeretina*	Quercus			Caucasus	WGSOS
Q. robur 'Kasseler Rakete'	Quercus				WOE
Q. robur 'Koster'	Quercus				TC
Q. robur 'Oxycantha'	Quercus				NOTO
Q. robur 'Pectinata'	Quercus				SDH
Q. robur subsp. *pedunculiflora*	Quercus			SE Europe-SW Asia	GHCF - TOW
Q. robur subsp. *pedunculiflora* 'Cankiri'	Quercus				OTCF
Q. robur Pendula Group	Quercus	Weeping oak			TC
Q. robur 'Pulverulenta'	Quercus				TOW
Q. robur 'Purpurascens'	Quercus				WOC
Q. robur 'Raba'	Quercus				WOC
Q. robur 'Rita's Gold'	Quercus				RRNE
Q. robur 'Salfast'	Quercus				WOE
Q. robur 'Strypemonde'	Quercus				TC
Q. robur var. *thomasii*	Quercus			Italy	WOC
Q. robur 'Totem'	Quercus				FBH
Q. robur 'Zeeland'	Quercus				WOC
Q. ×rosacea 'Columna'	Quercus		*Q. petraea × Q. robur*		RRSWT - TOE
Q. rotundifolia	Cerris			S Spain-S Portugal-N Africa	SDH - TC
Q. rubra	Lobatae	Red oak		E North America	ESD - FBH - OTCF - SP - TOW
Q. rubra Aurea Group	Lobatae				WGNOS
Q. rubra 'Cyrille'	Lobatae				WOE
Q. rubra 'Magic Fire'	Lobatae				RRP
Q. rubramenta	Lobatae			Guerrero, Mexico	GHB
Q. ×rudkinii	Lobatae		*Q. marilandica × Q. phellos*	E United States	RRP
Q. rugosa	Quercus	Netleaf oak		Mexico-SW United States	GHB - RRSWT - WOTO
Q. ×runcinata	Lobatae		*Q. imbricaria × Q. rubra*	E United States	RRNE - RRP
Q. rysophylla	Lobatae	Loquat oak		NE Mexico	ESD - RRP

NAME	GROUP	COMMON NAME	PARENTAGE	NATURAL RANGE	MAP LOCATIONS
Q. sadleriana	Quercus	Deer oak		N California-SW Oregon	ROCK - SP
Q. salicina	Cyclobalanopsis			S Japan-S Korea	ESD - WGSOS
Q. sapotifolia	Lobatae			Mexico-Guatemala	NOTO
Q. ×sargentii	Quercus		*Q. montana × Q. robur*		RRNE
Q. sartorii	Lobatae			Mexico	GHB - RRSWT - WGNOS - WOC
Q. ×saulii	Quercus		*Q. alba × Q.montana*	N America	FBH
Q. ×schochiana	Lobatae		*Q. palustris × Q. phellos*	E United States	GHCF
Q. schottkyana	Cyclobalanopsis			China	ESD - RRP - WGNOS - WGSOS
Q. ×schuettei	Quercus		*Q. bicolor × Q. macrocarpa*	Wisconsin	AO - GHCF - RRST
Q. semecarpifolia	Cerris			Himalaya-Tibet	RRP - RRSE - WOTO
Q. serrata	Quercus			Japan-Korea-China	RRSWT - WGNOS - WGSOS
Q. serrata var. *brevipetiolata*	Quercus			China-Japan	WOC
Q. serrata subsp. *mongolicoides*	Quercus			Japan	GHB
Q. sessilifolia	Cyclobalanopsis			China-Japan-Taiwan	GHCF
Q. shumardii	Lobatae	Shumard oak		E United States	RRP - WGSOS
Q. shumardii var. *schneckii*	Lobatae			C United States	OTCF
Q. sinuata	Quercus	Durand white oak		SE United States-North Mexico	RRNE
Q. sinuata subsp. *breviloba*	Quercus			Texas-North Mexico	GHCF
Q. 'Souvenir de Jacques Lombarts'	Lobatae				RRN - RRNE
Q. stellata	Quercus	Post oak		C & E United States	FBH
Q. stellata × Q. mohriana	Quercus				GHCF
Q. stenophylloides	Cyclobalanopsis			Taiwan	WOTO
Q. "sternbergii"	Lobatae		*Q. buckleyi × Q. shumardii*		GHCF - RRSE
Q. stewardiana	Cyclobalanopsis			Yunnan, China	GHB
Q. ×streimii 'Kortrijk'	Quercus		*Q. petraea × Q. pubescens*		KG
Q. ×streimii 'Lanze'	Quercus		*Q. petraea × Q. pubescens*		OTCF
Q. suber	Cerris	Cork oak		W Mediterranean region	GHCF - RRNE - SDH
Q. suber (purple-leaved form)	Cerris				RRN
Q. subspathulata	Quercus			Mexico	RRP
Q. ×tabajdiana	Quercus		*Q. frainetto × Q. petraea*	SE Europe	OTCF
Q. texana	Lobatae	Nuttall oak		S United States	SP - WGSOS - WOC - WOTO
Q. texana New Madrid Group	Lobatae				RRST
Q. tomentella	Protobalanus	Island live oak		Calif. Channel Is.-Guadalupe Is., Mexico	GHB - WGNOS
Q. ×tridentata	Lobatae		*Q. imbricaria × Q. marilandica*	Illinois-Missouri	RRNE
Q. trojana	Cerris	Macedonian oak		SE Italy-Turkey	AO - GHCF - NOTO - RRP - TOW
Q. trojana subsp. *euboica*	Cerris			Evia, Greece	GHCF
Q. tungmaiensis	Cerris			Tibet	NOTO
Q. turbinella × Q. lobata	Quercus				WOW
Q. ×turneri 'Gnom'	Cerris × Quercus		*Q. ilex × Q. robur*		GHCF
Q. ×turneri 'Pseudoturneri'	Cerris × Quercus		*Q. ilex × Q. robur*		RRST - SDH
Q. ×undulata 'Cimarron'	Quercus				RRSET
Q. ×undulata 'Pecos Monastery'	Quercus				WOC

NAME	GROUP	COMMON NAME	PARENTAGE	NATURAL RANGE	MAP LOCATIONS
Q. (unknown species)					GHB - GHCF - OTCF
Q. uxoris	Lobatae			Mexico	GHC
Q. vacciniifolia	Protobalanus	Huckleberry oak		California-Oregon-Nevada	ROCK
Q. variabilis	Cerris	Chinese cork oak		China-Japan-Korea	GHCF - RRP - WOC - WOE
Q. vaseyana	Quercus			Texas-North Mexico	GHCF - ROCK
Q. velutina	Lobatae	Black oak		E North America	RRP
Q. velutina 'Albertsii'	Lobatae				WOC
Q. velutina 'Habiflax'	Lobatae				WOC
Q. velutina 'Oakridge Walker'	Lobatae				RRSE
Q. velutina 'Rubrifolia'	Lobatae				WGNOS
Q. ×vilmoriniana	Quercus		*Q. dentata × Q. petraea*		RRNE - RRP
Q. virginiana	Quercus	Live oak		SE United States	RRP - WOTO
Q. vulcanica	Quercus			Turkey	RRSWT
Q. ×warburgii	Quercus	Cambridge oak	*Q. robur × Q. rugosa*		NOTO - WOE
Q. ×warei 'Windcandle'	Quercus		*Q. bicolor × Q. robur*		FBH
Q. wislizeni	Lobatae	Interior live oak		California	WGSOS - WOTO
Q. wislizeni var. *frutescens*	Lobatae			California	GHB
Q. wutaishanica	Quercus			NE Asia	SP
Q. xalapensis	Lobatae			E Mexico	GHB
Q. yunnanensis	Quercus			Yunnan-Sichuan	GHCF - RRNE - TOW
Q. 'Zehra'	Lobatae		*Q. falcata × Q. rysophylla*		RRST
LITHOCARPUS					
L. corneus				S China-Taiwan	NOTO
L. dealbatus				China	NOTO - RRNE
L. edulis				C & S Japan	WGNOS - WGSOS
L. glaber				S China-Taiwan	NOTO
L. hancei				S China-Japan-Taiwan	GHCF - NOTO - RRST
L. henryi				SW China	NOTO
L. kawakamii				Taiwan	GHCF - NOTO
L. konishii				Taiwan	GHCF
L. lepidocarpus				Taiwan	GHCF - NOTO
L. truncatus				China	NOTO
L. (unknown species)					GHB
L. variolosus				China	WOTO

Index

Only the names of the plants that are mentioned in the main text (pages 206–215) have been indexed here. Where the description is substantial the page number is in bold. Page references to illustrations are underlined.